Can't Help Singing

Music advisor to Northeastern University Press

GUNTHER SCHULLER

Can't Help Singing

THE LIFE OF EILEEN FARRELL

Eileen Farrell
and
Brian Kellow

Northeastern University Press
BOSTON

Northeastern University Press

Library of Congress Cataloging-in-Publication Data
Farrell, Eileen.
   Can't help singing : the life of Eileen Farrell / Eileen Farrell and Brian
Kellow.
      p. cm.
   Includes bibliographical references, discography (p.   ), and index.
   ISBN 1-55553-406-6 (alk. paper)
      1. Farrell, Eileen.   2. Sopranos (Singers)—United States
biography.   I. Kellow, Brian.   II. Title.
ML420.F275A3   1999
782'.0092—dc21
[B]   99-34401

Designed by Gary Gore

Composed in Bembo by Graphic Composition, Inc., Athens, Georgia. Printed and
bound by Quebecor Printing, Brattleboro, Vermont. The paper is Quebecor Liberty,
an acid-free sheet.

MANUFACTURED IN THE UNITED STATES OF AMERICA
03 02 01 00 99   5 4 3 2 1

To the memory of my mother and father

Contents

List of Illustrations

Acknowledgments

This book wouldn't have materialized without the support of many colleagues and friends. From the beginning, Helene Greece was enthusiastic about the idea and helpful in seeing that it got off the ground. Our agent, Robert Cornfield, has seen to numerous details that would have escaped us completely, and has done so with great care and professionalism. Bill Frohlich, our editor and the director at Northeastern University Press, has shown tremendous concern while the work has progressed. Thanks also to his assistant, Barbara Lenes, and to production director Ann Twombly for their attention to many matters.

We are grateful to Rudolph S. Rauch, editor and publisher of *Opera News,* who has supported this book every step of the way. Our thanks, too, to F. Paul Driscoll, managing editor of *Opera News,* for being a constant source of encouragement and information.

Other staff members of *Opera News*—Elizabeth Diggans, John W. Freeman, and Louise T. Guinther—read the manuscript and provided thoughtful comments. Edgar Vincent has offered valuable insights that made the job easier.

We received much-needed aid from Robert Tuggle, director of the Metropolitan Opera Archives, along with his assistant, John Pennino. Thanks also to the staffs of the Museum of Television and Radio, the New York Philharmonic Archives, and the Lincoln Center Library for the Performing Arts; and to David Lombard, CBS Photography; Kristine Krueger of the Margaret Herrick Library of the Academy of Motion Picture Arts and Sciences; Elena Park, press and public relations director for the Brooklyn Academy of Music; Elizabeth Connell, public relations manager for the San Francisco Opera; Kori Lockhart, director of publications and archivist of the San Francisco Opera; Mary L. Serantoni, of the press office of the Lyric Opera of Chicago; and Monte Jacobson, of the marketing and communications department of the Seattle Opera.

Individuals who helped in a variety of ways include Beth Bergman, Philip Campanella, Mrs. Curtis L. Farnsworth III, Patrick Giles, Sonya Haddad, Joel Honig, James M. Keller, Emily Kellow, Dr. Margery Lowens, Arlo McKinnon, Betsy Mingo, Laura Nichols, and Fred Plotkin.

And thanks to those who shared their memories: Ruth and Julius Baker, William Berdick, Barbara Carroll, Lili Chookasian, Emily Coleman, Barbara Cook, Gloria DeHaven, Sam Draper, Robert Farnon, John Farrell, Mary Lynn Fixler, Sue Anne Gershenson, Alice Ghostley, Bernard Greenhouse, Diann Thomas Harris, Dr. Stephen Harris, J. Tamblyn Henderson, Claramae Turner Hoffman, Bart Howard, Arge Keller, Sunny Joy Langton, Marvin David Levy, Dorothy Loudon, Loonis McGlohon, Gian Carlo Menotti, Robert Merrill, Mitch Miller, Kathan Kennedy Neal, Roberta Peters, André Previn, Esther Rauch, Robert Reagan, Jr., Charles Nelson Reilly, William Scheide, Beverly Sills, Risë Stevens, Blanche Thebom, George Trovillo, Margaret Whiting, Alix Williamson, Jack Wrangler.

Thanks to the following for their personal support: to Erik Dahl, who wanted this book to happen nearly as much as we did, and to Jack and Marjorie Kellow and Barry and Kami Kellow for lending a sympathetic ear—not only during the writing of this book, but always.

Finally, deepest gratitude to two people: Kathleen Reagan (a.k.a. Ophelia Pulse), a remarkable doctor, daughter, and friend, and Bill Braun, whose wit, patience, and understanding helped no end in filling the blank page.

Eileen Farrell
Brian Kellow
New York City
February 1999

Can't Help Singing

*I*N STORRS, Connecticut, where I lived when I was a child, our driveway connected with a long road that wound around the corner, and if you followed it for a little while, our house would disappear from sight. One day, when I was about five years old, I was playing outside; my mother and father and brother and sister were all busy inside the house, and no one was paying any attention to me. I was feeling a little restless, I guess, because I decided to go for a walk. I left the yard and wandered down the road.

I wasn't gone for very long, and when I came back, the whole family was out in the yard waiting for me. My parents were furious. My father cut a branch off a nearby bush and switched me across the back of my legs. I couldn't understand why they were so upset. I hadn't tried to run away from home, and I hadn't gotten lost; I'd just wanted to take a little walk. It's one of my earliest memories.

About fifteen years later, I was singing an audition in a studio at CBS Radio in Manhattan. The room was empty except for the pianist and me. On the opposite wall from where I stood, there was a huge window, and on the other side of it was the engineer and the CBS "suits." I sang the only aria I knew, "Vissi d'arte," and I can remember everything about that audition—the way the room smelled, the sound of my voice echoing off the walls, the way my hands shook. I was on my own in New York City, miles from home, and I was scared to death. I'd never really been anywhere, and now my parents had decided I was ready to go out into the world to see if I had what it takes to be a singer. I couldn't for the life of me figure out how I was going to make it, and I don't think I felt much more prepared to handle myself than I had when I took that solo walk down the driveway in Storrs.

But I did make it. Growing up, I didn't know much about life outside the little towns in Connecticut and Rhode Island where my family lived. Suddenly, I was singing on the radio, and then on recordings and eventually onstage. Thousands of strangers were watching me and listening to me. It's strange to think about—in fact, to this day it scares me to think about it too much, because I really don't have the faintest idea how it all happened.

A lot of it was thanks to my mother. I can still see myself singing "Fairy Gardens" or "Sylvia" with the band at my high school in Woonsocket, Rhode Island, and my mother sitting in the audience with her hands in her lap. She wouldn't have applauded me to save her life—she never did, not even twenty years later when I was singing at the Metropolitan Opera. It wasn't that she disapproved of me being onstage, because she was the one who encouraged my singing more than anyone else. She was afraid that people might think she was a little too proud of having a daughter who sang.

My mother, Catherine Felicita Kennedy, was born July 3, 1886, in Danielson, Connecticut. The Kennedys were a solid

Irish Catholic family, and music was a big part of my mother's life from the beginning. She sang, played the piano and organ, and was good at all three. When she was still young, her family moved to Woonsocket, where my Grandfather Kennedy owned a woolen mill. Kitty—as the family always called her—was a good student and went on to secretarial school. She also sang in the choir at our parish church, St. Charles Borromeo. Through a mutual friend in the choir, she met a handsome young fellow named Michael John Farrell. They met, fell in love, and on June 30, 1909, were married in that same church in Woonsocket.

Michael John Farrell was "show business" almost from the very beginning. He was born on November 3, 1886, in St. John's, Newfoundland. He was a boy soprano, and when he was ten years old, his parents allowed him to perform in public. He made his professional debut with the Frankie Stock Company, and pretty soon he was appearing quite often in vaudeville shows. Novelty acts were all the rage, and my father worked up a routine as a bird imitator. It was a big hit, and eventually he was billed as the "Irish Songbird." The vaudeville circuit at the turn of the century was pretty rowdy, and some of the roughnecks in one of the companies thought the "Irish Songbird" might sing even better if he was oiled up a little, so they started forcing whiskey down his throat before he went onstage. My mother always felt this was the start of the drinking problem he later developed.

All during his childhood, my father was busy appearing with stock and repertory companies along the East Coast. As he got older, he matured into a high baritone, and he started singing in silent movie theaters. I have a clipping from a 1910 newspaper from Norwich, Connecticut, announcing that week's movie at the Scenic Theatre: "The management has decided to repeat their former feature picture of last Saturday, *The Redman's Child*, a beautiful story of love, hatred and revenge. . . . M. J. Farrell will sing 'Hoo-Hoo, Ain't You Coming Out Tonight,' with a

My mother, Catherine Kennedy
Farrell, was a talented coloratura
soprano. Personal collection of
Eileen Farrell.

whistling chorus." And from the same newspaper: "The feature picture is *Behind the Scenes,* a story of a mother's love for her child. The picture is bound to get the people talking. . . . M. J. Farrell will sing 'When Sweet Marie Was Sweet Sixteen,' a beautiful ballad. Mr. Farrell sang this song three consecutive weeks in their Woonsocket house and made a decided hit at every performance."

After they got married, my parents formed their own vaudeville act. They were known as Farrell and Farrell, or sometimes as the Singing O'Farrells, and they sang everything from Mozart to traditional Irish songs. For a time they had something billed as an "Indian novelty act"—I'd give anything to have seen it, but they quit vaudeville long before I was born. The only remains of their touring days is a pile of tattered, yellowed clippings I have tucked away in a box. They didn't waste any time starting a family; my sister Leona Catherine was born in Woonsocket on May 21, 1910. Then came Gertrude, in 1913, and John Lowry, born in Amesbury, Massachusetts, on July 9, 1915. And on February 13, 1920, in Willimantic, Connecticut, I came along—Eileen Frances.

Kitty Kennedy was always the lady—quiet and hardworking, very disciplined, stoic, even-tempered, always holding her cards close to her chest. My father was the opposite who attracted—you couldn't miss him. Whenever a visitor dropped in, he'd break into a huge smile and call out, "Come on in—sit down and take a load off your hands and face!" It was a game with him to try to make my mother laugh, and all she usually gave him was a tight little smile. Once, when they were attending Mass together, my father's asthma began to bother him. He needed to get some fresh air, so he leaned over to my mother and told her he had to leave. "Hold this for me until after church," he whispered and he pressed something into her hand as he left the pew. She looked down and saw that he'd handed her his false teeth.

My father was very handsome, and always well dressed; I have a picture of him in a tuxedo made out of silk moiré. He was a real romantic, too—I remember how he used to sneak up behind my mother and smooch her, which drove her crazy—any big display of affection embarrassed her. But even though my mother didn't make a show of it, she loved my father deeply, and there were plenty of times when he put her love to the test.

My father was a binge drinker. He could leave liquor alone for three or four years, and then, without warning, off he'd go. Once in a while, I would see him staggering down the street, on his way home from a tavern. Often he didn't come home at night, and the next day at school, I'd hardly be able to concentrate on my studies, worrying that he'd come home drunk and embarrass me in front of my friends.

The worst of it had happened before I was born. My parents had lived for a time in Panama City, Florida, where my father had gotten a temporary job. One night, when he was out at one of his favorite local taverns, he fell into conversation with a bunch of strangers. They were very friendly, buying him round after round. He drank so much he finally passed out. Several hours later he woke up on a steamer and realized he'd been shanghaied—pressed into service on the ship. My mother was frantic. For a long time, she had no idea where he was, but eventually she got word from him. It was several months before he had worked enough to buy his passage back to Florida.

I didn't know about this episode until years later, when I was in junior high school. My father had just taken off on one of his sprees, and I was upset, so I thought I would hand out some advice to my mother.

"Why do you put up with him?" I asked her. "Why don't you leave him?"

"You don't have the slightest idea what you're talking about," she said.

She was right—I didn't have a clue, and it was a long time before I figured it out.

While my mother was alone in Panama City, wondering what had become of her husband, Gertrude contracted whooping cough. My mother had hired a local woman to help her around the house, and the woman spent hours transferring Gertrude between two tubs of water—one icy cold, the other steaming hot. This was what people did to treat typhoid and all kinds of diseases when they couldn't think of anything better. It didn't work for poor Gertrude any better than it worked for anyone else, and she died before her second birthday. My mother didn't tell me about Gertrude until years later, and I never heard my father mention her, ever. I can't imagine how guilty he must have felt over not being there to help my mother through such a terrible time.

My family moved around Connecticut quite a bit during my early years. Although I was born in Willimantic, at 101 North Street, the first house I can remember was in Storrs, just a few miles away. It belonged to Storrs Agriculture College (now the University of Connecticut), where both my parents were employed. My father taught dramatics, and my mother was director of the girls' glee club. She also played piano in local silent-movie houses. When I was five years old, we returned to Willimantic, where I attended first grade. Then my mother got a job as organist for St. Mary's Church in Norwich, and we moved again. Finally we stayed in one place for a little while; Norwich was home until my sophomore year in high school. By this time, my father, who was a talented artist, was making his living as a painter. He painted houses for the income but he developed a reputation for painting theaters. These were the days of the big old movie palaces, and my father decorated them in some very clever and complicated color schemes; he could also paint simulated wood grain on doors. Eventually, he became known for his work with gold leaf, and Warner Brothers hired him to paint many of the big theaters they owned. He was especially proud of the gold leaf design in New York's Paramount Theater on Broadway.

My mother's parents, Grandpa and Grandma Kennedy, were a big part of my life. My grandfather and I were particularly close. He was a quiet man with a big white handlebar moustache and a head so big he had to have his caps custom made. He had sold his woolen mill by the time I came along, and he and my grandmother had moved to Woonsocket. They lived at 239 Manville Road, in a big house on a hill that was the gathering place for the entire family, and would remain so for many years. A few yards away from the house, my grandfather built a little store, cut right into the side of the hill, where he sold cigars and cigarettes, canned goods, and penny candy. He also had a beautiful marble ice cream fountain, and on hot days, all the local kids poured in and out of his store. He was the king of Manville Road.

My grandparents had seven children—Aunt Etta, my mother, Aunt Leona, Uncle Harold, Uncle Charlie, Aunt Helen, and Uncle Ray. I'm still especially close to one of Uncle Ray's daughters, Kathan. My Auntie Leona unexpectedly left home when she was very young to enter the convent, where she became Sister Frances Cecilia and spent a long and rewarding life in the Order of Notre Dame de Namur. My Aunt Helen never married; she became a popular English teacher at Woonsocket Junior High School, where she worked for many years.

As a child, I was terribly shy, but the one person I could open up to was Grandpa Kennedy. We would sit for hours, just the two of us, on the glassed-in porch of his house in Woonsocket. I would tell him everything that was on my mind while he sat puffing on one of his cigars. He made me feel like the most important person in the world. The family claimed that Grandpa Kennedy had a sixth sense, and once he had an actual vision. When his daughter Leona decided to become a nun, she packed her bag and left the house early one morning without saying a word to anyone. My grandfather was devastated. He couldn't believe that his daughter would leave for the convent without telling him. He brooded over it for months. Then something happened to change his mind. As he told it, one morning he got up and was getting dressed when he happened to look out the bedroom window and see the Blessed Mother. He said she had a serene, gentle smile on her face. "I was so stunned," he told me years later, "that I instantly knew it was wrong for me to be angry with my little girl."

My father's parents had died long before I was born, but we did see quite a bit of my father's two sisters, Aunt Mary and Aunt Anna. Aunt Mary was an old-fashioned, very tightly wrapped Irish spinster who attended daily Mass. She made her living as head of the linen department at Shepard's, a large department store in Providence, Rhode Island, and she was simply *made* for the linen department—everything always had to be just so—neat as a pin.

Aunt Anna was more my speed. Almost everything she did or said came out wrong, but she kept blundering along, never giving a damn. Once she needed to have all her teeth pulled. Her dentist told her that in order for her gums to toughen and her mouth to heal more quickly, she would have to exercise it by chewing gum. Try as she might, she couldn't get the gum worked up, so she would give it to me. I would get it going, then give it back to Aunt Anna! Later, Aunt Anna met her match when she married my Uncle Irving. He had the strangest occupation I ever heard of: he manufactured satin linings for coffins!

My early childhood was the only time in my life that I've ever been thin. I was sick *all* the time. Chicken pox, mumps, diphtheria, all kinds of colds, and flu. When I was around ten, there was a scarlet fever epidemic, and I came down with that, too. The hospitals were filled, so my mother had to treat me at home. One ear was so infected she had to drain it twice a day with water from a hot water bottle. After I recovered, my whole body chemistry changed, and I suddenly became very healthy—and fat.

The Singing O'Farrells weren't in vaudeville anymore, but they still performed in churches, putting on plays and musicales. They would sing "Just a Song at Twilight" or some wonderful old Irish tune, with my mother at the piano. It's funny that I can't recall what my mother's voice sounded like, but I can still hear my father's high baritone. It was beautiful and strong, and a little sad. He sang straight from the heart, and the minute he opened his mouth, his voice took hold of me, and I would start to cry. There was some quality that got to me—just the way some people cry when they hear Roland Hayes or John McCormack. My father played banjo, guitar, and saxophone, too. Once he made a mandolin. It required a special kind of wood, and he was very proud of it; I can still see his long fingers strumming it as he sang. Unfortunately, after he went on one of his binges, the mandolin wound up in hock.

We all sang at home. Like my mother, my sister Leona had a lovely coloratura soprano voice. While the family was living in Panama City, Florida, before I was born, Leona made her stage debut singing "There's a Girl in the Heart of Maryland" at a local theater. "This was her first appearance on the stage," wrote *The Panama City Advertiser,* "but it would never have been known from the way she sang. The little lady reappeared both nights in the midst of applause that would have rattled many grown stage-folks and sang again as before."

I studied piano for about two summers, but I gave it up pretty quickly; I wasn't the kind of kid who stuck with anything for long. I continued to play a little, though. My mother subscribed

That's me in my preschool days,
before the nuns got hold of me.
Personal collection of Eileen Farrell.

to *Musical America,* which in those days published songs in each issue. I would sit at the piano having a great time sight-reading, although I was stumped by anything with more than three flats.

Reporters used to ask me, "When was the moment when you realized you were going to be a singer?" I never knew what to say—maybe the day I got my first paycheck from CBS Radio? Lots of singers like to tell you that they were sitting at a performance of *Aida* when they were ten years old, and right in the middle of "O patria mia" they had an out-of-body experience and just *knew* they were meant to sing. Well, nothing like that ever happened to me. Music was just part of my everyday family life, and singing was something I always did. I do, however, remember my stage debut. It was in the second grade, and my mother staged the St. Mary's school pageant. I was cast as a raindrop and wore a green crepe-paper costume.

As a youngster, my steadiest gig was singing with my brother, John, in the choir at St. Mary's Church. (My mother had volunteered our services.) Occasionally, my mother would play for a funeral, and I would be excused from class in order to sing the Waiting Hymn that was always sung at the conclusion of Mass. I remember one funeral in particular. I was singing "When Evening Comes," a very somber hymn. Suddenly, a tall man in one of the front pews leaped up and screamed, "STOP! STOP!" I *did* stop—cold. The man's eyes were wild; he was truly overcome with grief. He looked up at me and shouted, "DON'T SING THAT ANYMORE!" His voice bounced off the cold church walls. I was stunned—I thought he hated my singing—and I burst into tears. My mother, playing the organ, leaned over, patted my arm, and whispered, "It's all right—calm down." Then, nonchalantly, she started in on another hymn as if nothing had happened.

In Norwich, we had a radio in the living room. I fantasized about being a dancer, and I would turn on the radio, close the doors, and dance around the living room to my favorite pop tunes. We listened to the radio a lot—*the Shadow, Myrt and Marge, Amos 'n' Andy.* Best of all were the prizefight broadcasts. It amazes me to think that my ladylike mother encouraged us to listen to a fight, but she seemed to enjoy it as much as anyone. She would make a pot of fudge, and we would sit around listening to Jack Dempsey and Joe Johnson duking it out. Of course, I didn't have the slightest idea what I was hearing. Once the announcer said that one fighter feinted with his right, and I got up and said, "Oh, good! He *fainted*! It's over!" On Saturday afternoons, Leona was always planted in front of the radio, listening to the Metropolitan Opera broadcasts. She couldn't get enough of *La Bohème* and *Aida,* but I thought they were awful.

Even more than the radio, I loved the movies. In the early '30s, *Dr. Jekyll and Mr. Hyde* came out, with Fredric March and Miriam Hopkins. I was desperate to see it, but my mother told me that under no circumstances was I to go. One afternoon, I sneaked off to the local movie theater where *Dr. Jekyll* was playing. But I didn't get away with it for long. That night in bed, I was afraid to go to sleep. When I started to cry, my mother came in. "You went to the movie, didn't you?" she said. I was grounded for weeks.

One of my favorite movies from childhood was the big Warner Brothers musical *42nd Street,* with its snappy songs and splashy dance numbers. But the one I remember best is *Tarzan, the Ape Man.* I couldn't have cared less about Johnny Weismuller's muscles, but I couldn't get over the movie's background score. It's the first time I remember being aware of the power music could have. When the movie ended, I decided to sit through the next show, just to listen to the music again—until my father showed up at the theater to remind me that dinner was ready.

One day I was at the dentist, having a tooth pulled. The dentist's office was on the second floor, and it overlooked a bank. Suddenly there was a big commotion outside. I looked out the window. People were running around in a panic and yelling like crazy. I wondered what was wrong, and pretty soon word came that President Roosevelt had ordered the banks closed. For the rest of the decade, my father had a much harder time getting work painting houses. Fortunately, my mother kept us going through hard times with the little bit she made as a church organist.

When I was growing up, both before and during the Depression, we faced a constant struggle for money. We lived simply, yet I didn't think we were missing much. Many times, meals were just the bare essentials, without any meat. One of my mother's standbys was carrots and potatoes and onions, all boiled and mashed up. For dessert, sometimes she'd cook rice with raisins and brown sugar, but much of the time, we did without. Since we'd never had much, it didn't occur to us to complain.

I do remember that once I was hit very hard by how poor we were. It was Christmastime, and Leona, John, and I were looking forward to decorating the tree with the ornaments we had saved from year to year. But my mother told us that she didn't have the twenty-five cents to buy a Christmas tree that year. John and I hung the ornaments over pictures and strung them up over the fireplace, trying to act like it didn't matter. That was the worst Christmas of my life.

One day when we were living in Storrs, my mother and father took Leona, John, and me out for a walk. Leona didn't want to go, and my mother said, "One of these days, you'll want to walk, and you won't be able to." I don't think my mother was a superstitious person, but years later, she always blamed herself for saying that.

When Leona was fifteen, she got up one morning and set off for school, dressed in her gym uniform, wearing the long, black

My sister Leona, August 1914,
Panama City, Florida. Leona had
a tough life, and more guts than
anyone I've ever known. Personal
collection of Eileen Farrell.

silk stockings that all girls were required to wear in 1925. As she got on the school bus, she scraped her instep, ripping the hose and cutting her foot. At first she didn't pay much attention to it, but she developed a widespread infection leading up to water on the knee. The doctors put her in casts, but they were left on too long. When the casts were finally removed, the joints of Leona's entire lower body—hips, knees, ankles, toes—were completely fused. It was as if she was frozen solid from the waist down. My parents were devastated. For years, Leona was in and out of Hartford Hospital. During this time she was in constant agony. The nurses would help her out of bed, but the moment her feet touched the floor, she would feel excruciating pain and lose consciousness.

I'll always remember a wonderful family who were our land-lords at the time. Mr. and Mrs. Solomon lived next door. They owned a grain and seed company and were quite well-off. The Solomons had a big Cadillac, and every Sunday, they would drive my mother and me to Hartford to see Leona at the hospital.

It was a long trip without much of a payoff for me, since children weren't allowed to visit. I missed Leona and wanted so much to see her. Instead, my mother went up while I sat alone downstairs. There was nothing to do, and sometimes I was afraid, sitting there by myself in such a strange place. But I kept my eyes open, and before long I was studying the faces—the tough faces of the nurses who marched by, matter-of-factly going about their business, and the haggard faces of people coming to call on their sick friends and relatives. I'd overhear bits of conversation and try to imagine what these people's lives must be like. Years later, I told Leonard Bernstein this story. It turned out that a relative of Lenny's had been confined to the mental hospital in Danvers, Massachusetts. When Lenny was a child, his mother and father would go for weekend visits, taking him along and leaving him alone in the lobby. "I know exactly how you must have felt, Eileen," Lenny said.

When Leona finally came home from the hospital, she was unable to climb stairs. She slept in a special bed that my parents had set up in the living room. John and I had to take care not to disturb Leona when she was resting, so we were forced to be quiet and well-behaved; we learned to discipline ourselves.

Leona must have inherited my mother's disposition. I never heard her cry or complain once. I remember helping her climb the concrete steps leading up to my grandfather's house in Woonsocket. She couldn't bend at all, so I would put my arm around her, wedge my hip against her thigh and lift her from one step to the next. Eventually, Leona learned to walk with crutches and later a cane. More than anything, she wanted to be independent, and she learned to drive a car that was specially outfitted for her. It was very unusual for anyone in the mid–1950s, let alone a woman, to do this, since very few concessions were made to the handicapped at that time. She even got a job as a clerk in the accounting department of the Taft-Pierce Manufacturing Company in Woonsocket, where she worked for fifteen years.

It was sad that Leona's illness kept her from having a family of her own, because she adored children. She collected children's books, and over the years she introduced her nieces and nephews to many of the classics, including *Madeline, Ferdinand the Bull* and Dr. Seuss's books. She loved to read herself, and always filled the house with the best magazines—*The New Yorker, Harper's Bazaar, Vogue.* Old snapshots of her show a striking, bright-eyed woman; you would take her for someone who hadn't missed a thing in life. No question about it, she had more guts than anybody I've ever known.

My mother didn't really push me, but at the same time she knew I should have some decent exposure to music. After that, I could make my own decision about whether it was the right thing for me. We would practice scales over and over, working until all the notes were as even as possible. At first, it was difficult for me to sing them quickly. "Don't get excited about it," my mother would say calmly. "You'll get it. We'll try it another day."

I wonder now if she had some idea that I might have the makings of a major career. She never would have told me, though. She wouldn't have put that kind of pressure on me. She led me out very slowly. I was certainly the last one in the world to think I was going to make a career out of singing. Looking back, I guess I'm lucky that my mother encouraged me in music as much as she did, because I can't imagine what else I would have been fit for.

CHAPTER TWO

WHEN I WAS growing up in Norwich, the Catholic Church played a big part in my family's life. We didn't just rattle off the Our Fathers and Hail Marys and Acts of Contrition by rote. We broke them down, one line at a time, until we had a real understanding of what we were saying. The month of May is the Blessed Virgin Mary's month. Every night after dinner, throughout May, our family knelt down in the dining room and said the rosary. This was something all devout Catholic families were expected to do.

I was taught early on that one thing that separates Roman Catholics from Protestants is our belief that the Pope is infallible in matters of church doctrine. It may not matter whether I like a certain Pope, or think much of the changes he may institute. His infallibility is something Catholics are taught to accept completely. I'm afraid I'm pretty much a traditionalist when it comes to the Church. I don't believe women should be priests; I don't even like to see altar girls.

My patience with Church affairs was put to the test in the

1960s, when Vatican II came along. With these changes, the altar was turned around, with the priest facing and closer to the congregation. The Masses were now given in English instead of Latin. There were "God is Love" posters up everywhere. To me, all this practically ruined the Catholic ritual—there was no tradition and no mystery left. Pope John XXIII had decided that the Mass had to play to more of the people more of the time.

One Sunday, I was attending Mass in our parish at the Church of Our Lady of Good Counsel on Staten Island. I was miserable. I had been fighting with myself and lots of other people about the wisdom of all these changes. As the Mass went along in English, I sat there fuming, holding tight to the missal I'd carried around for years. Even if I didn't understand every Latin word, I'd always been able to follow the English translation that ran opposite. I turned a page. Suddenly I read the lines, "Sing to the Lord a new song, for He has done wondrous deeds." A shiver went straight up my spine. What had I been so angry about? "Sing to the Lord a new song." After that, I decided to stop making trouble about all the changes.

I attended first grade at a public school in Willimantic. The following year, when we moved to Norwich, I started in Catholic school. I had been raised strictly, but I didn't really know the meaning of discipline until I came face-to-face with the Sisters of Mercy at Saint Mary's School.

During school, the Sisters ran the show. It would never have *occurred* to most of us to question anything they told us to do. "Because Sister said so"—that was all we needed to hear, and we fell in line. If a student gave them any trouble, the Sisters of Mercy had their ways of enforcing discipline. They wore huge, black, sweeping habits bound at the waist with a broad leather belt looped through a big black ring with brown rosary beads hanging from it—and that belt was there to be used.

My first teacher at Saint Mary's was Sister Ivan. Since my mother was the church organist, Sister Ivan expected me to be an especially good girl. But I *wasn't* a very good girl. In fact, I seemed to be a born liar. I loved to make up stories, and I never seemed to learn that I would eventually be found out. One time the students were given books of raffle tickets to sell. I was eager to get on Sister Ivan's good side, so one day, while we were lined up ready to march out of school, I told her my father had bought up all my raffle tickets. Sister Ivan was so happy, and for a couple of days, I was her pet student. Of course, my father hadn't coughed up the money for a single ticket, and soon enough Sister Ivan demanded to see the money. When I came up empty-handed, she lectured me on the sin of lying and suspended me for a week. Before long, Saint Mary's hired my mother to teach weekly music lessons, which made it easier for her to keep an eye on me.

Crazy nun stories are something most Catholics have in common, and I've got mine. It wasn't long after I entered the fifth grade at Saint Mary's that I realized our homeroom teacher was a little loosely wrapped. I can't even remember her name; I only remember what we called her—"Sister God-Help-Us." The poor woman was just plain nuts. Every once in awhile, Sister God-Help-Us would come apart at the seams. One day, she lost it seconds before my mother was scheduled to teach our music class. Just as my mother was coming through the classroom door, Sister God-Help-Us hurled a pair of scissors at a child who had done something to upset her. The scissors sailed over the heads of the students in the front row, just missing my mother's head as she came through the door, and bounced off the chalkboard. Sister God-Help-Us wasn't at the school very long after that; I think she was too much even for the Sisters of Mercy.

For the next few years, I barely squeaked through school, skipping my homework, getting lousy grades, and constantly winding up in trouble. I had a fairly long rap sheet by the time I got to the seventh grade and came under the supervision of an especially formidable nun, Sister Andretta, or as we called her behind her back, "Sister And-We-Dread-Her." Sister Andretta had a face that could freeze water at a single glance. She didn't seem to have encountered anyone as dumb as I was before, and she called in my mother to tell her she was going to hold me back a grade. This hurt my mother terribly, because nobody in her family had ever been held back. She was concerned about the reaction of one person in particular. Over and over, she asked, "What am I going to tell Auntie Sister Frances?"

We hadn't seen much of Auntie Sister Frances after she became a nun. Hers was a very strict, secluded order, and one of the rules was that the nuns could rarely leave the convent. The only time I can remember Auntie Sister Frances coming home was when my grandparents died; even then, she had to return to the convent right away. These were the days when most nuns couldn't walk down the street unless they were in pairs and couldn't go to anyone's house unless someone happened to be sick. Leona, of course, was terribly ill, so a parade of nuns beat a steady path in and out of our house.

Auntie Sister Frances's other name was Cecilia, after the patron saint of music. It was an ideal choice for her, since she immersed herself in music and eventually wound up teaching violin, harp, and organ. For many years she taught at the Notre Dame Academy for Girls, in Boston. The curate of the school was a priest named Father Spellman, who later became the famous Cardinal Spellman of Saint Patrick's Cathedral in New York City. He was very fond of Auntie Sister Frances. Once, Leona needed mastoid surgery. Auntie Sister Frances knew that Father Spellman's brother was an ear, nose, and throat doctor, so she called Father Spellman and asked if his brother would perform the operation. The brother agreed, and the surgery was a success. After that, Father Spellman got to be pretty chummy with our entire family. When he returned from a trip to Rome, he'd often bring gifts for Auntie Sister Frances and my mother.

Later, Auntie Sister Frances was transferred to a convent in Fairfield, Connecticut, where she almost singlehandedly furnished the novitiate. This was in the heyday of S&H Green Stamps. When Auntie Sister Frances asked for donations to the church, many people gave her their stamp books. She would accumulate the stamp books in boxes and baskets until she could fill the back of the convent's station wagon with books. Then she would drive down to the local S&H store and march through, asking, "How much is that couch? How many books for that chair?" By the time she was finished, she had purchased another roomful of furniture with green stamps. News of Auntie's savvy with Green Stamps must have gotten around, because she was appointed treasurer for the entire order.

When Auntie Sister Frances died, when she was in her seventies, my family and I attended her funeral in Bridgeport, Connecticut. I remember the shock of walking into the room where her body was on view—no flowers, just a plain pine box, like something out of an old John Wayne movie.

CHAPTER THREE

*I*N 1935 I STARTED high school at the Norwich Free Academy. By the end of the school year, my family decided it was time to move again. My grandfather had just died in Woonsocket (Grandmother died some years earlier), and Aunt Helen and Aunt Etta had been living in my grandfather's house. Aunt Helen was busy teaching, and apparently Aunt Etta wasn't much help to her. It was decided that the Farrells would move north, and my mother would take charge of the household. That spring, we moved to the old house at 239 Manville Road. I think my mother was glad to be back in Woonsocket. Hardly a day passed that we didn't see or hear from some member of the family.

In the fall of 1936, I entered Woonsocket High. Unfortunately, the new school didn't make me a better student. I enjoyed history, art, and languages—I studied French, Italian, and Latin—but otherwise, it was "Goodnight, Irene." I was hopeless in biology, and it didn't help that I had a horrible crush on my teacher. Instead of listening to him as he explained how to classify plants,

I would sit and dream up all kinds of romantic fantasies. Soon enough, he got married. I was furious. For weeks I couldn't even look at him and I wished him only the worst. Then his wife got pregnant, and the poor thing died in childbirth, along with the baby. There was a traditional Irish wake in the family's home, and Aunt Helen and I went. I will never forget the sight of my teacher's wife lying in her coffin, in her wedding dress, with her baby by her side. I went home and cried for days. I was sure I'd brought about her death, and it was a long time before anyone could persuade me otherwise.

When I was in high school I was still very shy, and the thing I dreaded most of all was English class, where once a week we practiced public speaking. We were supposed to pick our own subject and give a talk about it. Oh, God—how I hated that class! Day after day, I tried to avoid eye contact with the teacher, hoping she wouldn't call on me. Finally, when there were only a few weeks of school left, I knew I was going to have to find something, *anything,* to talk about. I had read a magazine article that described how Campbell's soup was manufactured, and so help me God, I chose that as my topic. I'm not sure anyone was awake by the time I finished.

I was still taking voice lessons from my mother, who had been careful to let my voice develop slowly and naturally. We had a wonderful band at Woonsocket High, and I began to sing with them at school programs. Two of my big hits were "Sylvia" and "Trees." During my junior year, I played Buttercup in the school's production of Gilbert and Sullivan's *H.M.S. Pinafore.* Everyone told me I had a nice voice, but I figured they were just being polite.

During my senior year, the Woonsocket High band entered a statewide competition; I sang "Sylvia" and won the singing prize. That was the only voice contest I ever entered in my life. By the spring of 1939, I was a few weeks from graduating, and

I still didn't have the slightest idea what I was going to do with my life. I'd never had so much as a summer job. My grades were lousy right to the end. When graduation day finally came, I marched up the aisle, positive someone would block my way and tell me I'd flunked. But somehow I made it.

I guess I had some vague idea of looking for a job once fall came, and I was content to spend the summer seeing my friends and going to the movies. Around the end of July, my mother told me about a plan she obviously had been hatching for some time. Every Sunday, my parents bought *The New York Times,* and one Sunday morning, my mother noticed an advertisement placed by a singing teacher named Merle Alcock. When my mother was young, she had spent her summers in Hyannisport, on Cape Cod, where she studied voice with a woman named Ella Backus-Behr. She liked Mme. Backus-Behr's ideas about singing—she believed in letting the voice develop naturally—and since Merle Alcock had studied with Ella Backus-Behr, too, my mother figured she'd be the perfect teacher for me. She made an appointment for me to go to New York to audition for Mme. Alcock during the last week in August. That gave her the rest of the summer to scrape up enough money for the trip. I was thrilled: I had never been to New York in my life, and now I'd finally get to spend a few days in the city. Apart from that, I didn't give the matter much thought at all.

When that last week in August finally arrived, my mother and I got ready to leave for New York. The cheapest route was by boat, so we sailed from Providence and got to Manhattan early in the morning. Everything that happened that day is still clear in my mind. It was a warm late-summer morning, and we went uptown to see a show at Radio City Music Hall. Watching the giant organ rise up from the stage was the greatest thrill I'd ever had, and I started to cry. Afterward, we rode on the upper level of an open, double-decker bus to the Metropolitan Opera

House, at Thirty-ninth Street and Broadway. So this was where they did all those damned operas that made Leona hog the radio every Saturday afternoon! I didn't see anything impressive about this dirty old yellow brick building, but my mother caught my hand as we stood across the street looking at it and said, "Well . . . maybe. Someday."

Finally, we went down to Merle Alcock's studio on Fifth Avenue and Tenth Street. I don't remember what I sang—probably either "Sylvia" or "Trees." I must have been all right, because at the end of the audition, Mme. Alcock said she would accept me as her pupil.

By this time my brother, John, had graduated from the Vesper George School of Art in Boston and was working at Towle Silver Company designing flatware. He gave me $500 for my start-up money in New York. Soon I was off to Manhattan. It's funny to think about now. Here was someone so dumb that she didn't make it out of high school until she was nineteen, about to go off by herself to New York. Fortunately, I was so naïve I didn't have sense enough to be scared of what I was facing.

Merle Alcock suggested that I stay at the Evangeline, a twenty-floor hotel for girls run by the Salvation Army, at 123 West Thirteenth Street. You were admitted if you had a financial need. Most of the girls who lived there were studying to be secretaries. I had a little room to myself, with the bathroom down the hall. It was miserably hot, and the Evangeline didn't furnish electric fans. There was a big dining hall where the girls were seated six to a table, which forced us to talk to each other. A cafeteria-style breakfast and a sit-down dinner were included in the price of a room, which was eleven dollars a week. There was a parlor on the second floor, where the girls could entertain friends, and a big sewing room with four machines and a wall of mirrors, so the girls could check their work as they sewed. In the basement were several practice rooms with pianos, and there was a huge swimming pool, too. The Evangeline closed its doors at midnight. If you were out after that, you had to ring the bell to be admitted. The next morning, you were called in to the manager's office to explain why you were out late. It was a wonderful place, but when I got there, I was so afraid of everybody that I wouldn't even set foot in the dining hall for the first couple of weeks.

The Evangeline was only a few blocks away from Merle Alcock's studio—which was a good thing, because I was also terrified to go into the subway. When I began my lessons, we did exercises and scales, and she had me studying German, which I didn't know at all. I was miserable every single minute. I was afraid of Merle Alcock, I was afraid to go out on the street by myself, I was afraid to look anyone in the eye. I missed my family so much. At night, I lay in that stuffy room at the Evangeline, crying myself to sleep. At the end of the first week, I called my mother and told her I didn't think I could stay in New York.

"You'll have to stay," she said. "Just for a while. You haven't been there long enough to know whether you like it or not."

I burst into tears and carried on until my mother said she would come down from Rhode Island so we could talk it over face-to-face. When she arrived at the Evangeline, she was gentle but firm. She wanted me to study with Merle Alcock for at least one year. Then, if I still hated it, we would see what else to do. I saw how much faith she had in me. I thought about what it would be like to go through life knowing I had disappointed her, and I thought about how she had kept the family together through hard times. I wondered if life had taken her as far as she wanted to go. Had singing Juliette's Waltz at little music clubs and lodges been enough for her? I made up my mind: If she believed in me so much that she was willing to stake me to a year in New York, I'd hang on somehow.

My biggest challenge was Merle Alcock. She was a very

glamorous woman in her mid-fifties, with jet-black hair and beautiful ivory skin. When she taught, she always wore huge, dramatic caftans, which gave her an imposing presence. Although she never had been an important singer, she was a solid, reliable contralto who had sung lots of concert and oratorio engagements. During ten years, she had sung more than thirty comprimario roles at the Met. She may never have been a real prima donna on the stage, but off it she definitely knew how the part went. My time with her was one of the strangest apprenticeships any young singer ever had.

One day she asked me if I knew how to sew. I said yes, my mother had taught me to sew as a child. Before long I was sewing outfits for her. Another time she asked me if I knew how to cook. I said, yes, my mother had taught me to cook, too. Soon I was baking pies for her. From time to time, I did her ironing. But it didn't occur to me to complain. I didn't know any of Merle's other voice students. For all I knew, they worked under similar arrangements.

It wasn't long before I figured out that Merle didn't *have* any other students. Nobody came in, and nobody went out. But I was stuck. I didn't have the name of any other teacher in New York, and even if I had, I wouldn't have had the nerve to leave Merle, who intimidated me from the get-go. Once I showed up in a cotton dress. "Never," she said in a tone that almost made my heart stop, *"never* show up in *my* studio wearing a cotton dress again!" She sat simmering while I ran home to change. I'll say this about Merle, though: She used methods that enabled me to sing naturally. She may not have taught me a whole lot I didn't know already, but at least she didn't do me any harm.

I hung on in New York for about six months, until my money ran out. Then I returned to Woonsocket and went to Father Holland, the pastor at St. Charles Borromeo Church, and he agreed to stake me to a little more time in New York. My mother cashed in an insurance policy, and that helped. Back I went. Merle had an invalid sister living over on Twelfth Street, so I moved in with her for a time, getting her meals and running errands for her, and sleeping on a cot in her living room.

When the money ran out again, I was back in Woonsocket, where I got a job as a salesgirl at the Bluebird, a little shop that sold ladies' accessories. I was grateful that I didn't have to make change, because I wouldn't have had the faintest idea how to do it. (Recently I found a pay receipt for a single day's work at the Bluebird in 1940: It came to $2.63.) I enjoyed being home and seeing family and old friends, but New York had worked its way into my system. Although I still didn't have any real clue that I'd ever be able to make my living as a singer, I knew I wanted to go back.

It wasn't long before I got my chance. During the previous year, Merle Alcock had recommended me to Lucile Singleton at CBS Radio. Lucile was a very proper, well-groomed southern lady in charge of casting at CBS. All of the network's potential talent, even the people auditioning for soap operas, had to be screened by Lucile. I had done a general audition for her and hadn't heard anything more about it. But Lucile remembered me, and several months later she telephoned me in Woonsocket to ask if I could come back for another audition, for the CBS radio chorus.

"Thank you, Miss Singleton," I said. "But I'm sorry, I don't have the money to get to New York."

"That's all right, Miss Farrell," said Lucile. "We would very much like to hear you again. We'll wire you the money for the trip."

So off I went. I sang "The Last Rose of Summer" in an empty studio—just the pianist and me. Listening over the loudspeaker were Lucile and James Fassett, an announcer who would soon be made head of CBS's music department. Not long after the audition, I was told that I had landed my first professional singing job—a spot in the CBS chorus.

I came home, quit my job at the Bluebird, and checked back into the Evangeline. Now that I had a regular salary, I could afford a larger room, which I would share with another girl. I was thrilled to be back in New York, this time with a real job, paying my own way. My new room was on the eleventh floor. I arrived in the middle of the day and was told that my new roommate's name was Olive Green. No kidding. I went over to the window and opened it to see what kind of a view I had. Then I looked down at the floor and screamed bloody murder. Propped up behind a chair was somebody's leg. It turned out that Olive Green had an artificial leg, and for some reason she didn't feel like taking it to work that day. I found out soon enough that Olive's handicap didn't hold her back one bit. She went out dancing every single night—and not many nights did she come back!

I continued my lessons with Merle. When I was studying a particular art song, she made me write out the words five times. I hated it; it was like being back in school. But again, I did as I was told. At the Evangeline, I would lie in bed at night, when everything had quieted down, going over each song, line by line, until I could remember the whole thing.

I worked at CBS's headquarters, at 485 Madison Avenue. When I arrived, CBS had been around for only about ten years. William Paley had bought a struggling network of sixteen affiliates called United Independent Broadcasters and in a short time had expanded it into the Columbia Broadcasting System, which had gotten big enough to make NBC nervous. Bing Crosby had become a household name on CBS, and so had Kate Smith, Morton Downey, and Orson Welles, with his *Mercury Theatre of the Air*. I was a little awed by the place, and figured it was only a matter of time before I got fired, especially since I had one slight handicap for a singer: I couldn't read music very well. Fortunately, I was blessed with a good ear. So when the notes went up, I went up, and when the notes went down, I did the same.

The chorus job paid a little over fifty dollars a week. Finally, I was able to earn my own way and even send a little money home. In addition to the regular choral work, occasional odd jobs came up. At this point, my CBS contract was nonexclusive. In October 1941, Lucile Singleton called me in and told me that NBC was looking for someone to imitate Rosa Ponselle's voice on *The March of Time*. Ponselle was my idol. I never thought we sounded anything alike, but evidently someone did, because I was assigned to sing several bars of "Home Sweet Home," trying to sound as much like Ponselle as possible, on *The March of Time*.

Back then, everything was live. Even the popular serials— *The Romance of Helen Trent, Our Gal Sunday, Ma Perkins, Just Plain Bill*—used live music, and the kids in the chorus had all the work they could handle, running from one show to another. I probably never had any business being in the chorus at all. My voice wasn't as powerful as it later became, after I'd gotten some good training, but even then, I'm afraid it was LOUD. I spent three months deafening all the other kids in the chorus before Jim Fassett figured out that this wasn't the ideal spot for me. By then, Jim had become head of the music department at CBS, and he and Lucile Singleton asked me to go through another series of auditions. I was afraid they were doing a quality check and were going to give me the heave-ho. I sang "Vissi d'arte" at several auditions, with just my pianist, the engineer, and me. Again, the sound was piped downstairs, where Jim Fassett was listening, but this time he'd called in some of the other top executives at CBS to listen with him. Apparently I was OK, because one day Jim called me into his office and offered me my own half-hour program with the CBS Symphony, Howard Barlow conducting.

And that was the last time in my life I ever had to audition for anything. I can hardly believe it when I read about the rejection Maria Callas suffered when she was trying to get her career off the ground. With so many blows to the ego, how could she have kept going? Thank God I didn't have to contend with that, ever. There I was, a green kid from New England with practically no experience, about to star in her own radio show. You would think I'd have been terrified, but I wasn't. Strange as it sounds, singing was the one thing that *didn't* frighten me.

Merle Alcock suggested I get some language coaching and sent me to her friend Charlie Baker, a marvelous musician who had an apartment in the Ansonia Hotel on Seventy-third and Broadway. Charlie was also music director of Rutgers Presbyterian Church, right across the street from the Ansonia. He knew more about oratorio literature than anyone I've ever known, and before long, he'd given me a job as soloist for Sunday services.

And so, in 1941, *Eileen Farrell Sings* went on the air at 11:30 P.M. I was in good hands: Jim Fassett chose the program for my show every week. I always sang one aria, one art song—usually German or French—and one number in English. In between, the CBS Symphony would play two selections on its own. The programs were arranged in thirteen-week cycles, and I learned them three weeks in advance to make sure I had them under my belt.

Jim Fassett had an uncanny sense of what was right for my voice, and I learned to have absolute faith in his judgment. I also developed a terrible crush on him. Jim was drop-dead handsome, with a sexy voice and a Boston accent. He always wore a tweed jacket and smoked a pipe, and looked like he'd just stepped right off a college campus. If I'd stopped to think about exactly what I was doing, I probably would have panicked and taken the next train back to Woonsocket. But Jim believed in me, and I felt I had to live up to his expectations. I would take the assignments he gave me and go to Charlie Baker for coachings two or three times a week. I was soaking up new pieces like crazy, and I loved every second of it. I didn't think I was making great art. The radio show was just my job—and a damned good one.

Several of the thirteen-week segments were done in what's now the Ed Sullivan Theater. The wonderful engineers at CBS taught me so much about the technical end of singing for radio. I was no crooner; my voice was so big that it gave the boys in the control room fits. The needle was supposed to fall in the middle of the dial, but I'd open my mouth and knock it all the way to the right. The engineers were always coming up with ways to get me away from the microphone. They would listen to me and tell me to move to the right or left during my high notes. Sometimes, in some of the bigger studios, there would be mikes placed in various sections of the orchestra, and my voice would pick up on them, creating a lot of feedback, so I would have to stand behind a screen when I sang. All of these problems had to be worked out by air time.

The CBS Symphony was made up of the most terrific group of guys I'd ever met. Julius Baker was first flutist; he was (and still is) one of the funniest men in the world, and he used to say the most outrageous things in his quiet little voice, completely deadpan, just like a Borscht Belt comedian. Mitch Miller was oboist. Bernard Greenhouse was first cellist. They all loved to tell dirty jokes. I don't think any of them were too wild about our conductor, Howard Barlow. He was very bossy and condescending, and he was not a good enough conductor to get away with it.

In the 1940s, no one at CBS thought twice about smoking in front of a singer; so I sat there at rehearsals with all the guys puffing away on their cigarettes and cigars, and I don't think it hurt me one bit. For meals and rehearsal breaks, they started asking me to join them at Colbee's, the coffee shop in the CBS building. I discovered something surprising—I was starting to feel right at home with these people. They were funny and bright and talented, and they seemed to accept me as one of their own. Little by little, I was loosening up.

One look from Merle Alcock, however, could still freeze me solid. It was hard for me to tell if I was making any progress or not, because Merle never gave me much in the way of detailed musical criticism. She had plenty to say about my weight, though, and was always nagging me to slim down. Merle was a shrewd woman: She had figured out that maybe this little dummy from the sticks had a lot more potential than she had originally guessed. She persuaded me that since I was so naïve about business matters, she should act officially on my behalf. One week I went for a lesson and she presented a document for my signature. It read,

"Dear Mme. Alcock: I am entering into this agreement with you because I have thoroughly considered the advisability of appointing you my exclusive personal representative in all professional engagements. You agree to use your best efforts to create a demand for my services, and it is further agreed that in consideration of your efforts on my behalf, I shall pay you ten percent (10%) of my gross earnings for a term of three years from this date."

Of course, it is insane for any student to make this kind of deal with her teacher. But I was afraid to say no, so I signed it. Obviously, Merle suspected I might be capable of great things. As early as March 1940, she had arranged an audition for me with Edward Johnson, general manager of the Metropolitan Opera. I sang "Vissi d'arte." He made only two comments on my audition card, "Amateurish—fat." I couldn't have cared less. Who needed opera? I was having a ball at CBS.

Still, Jim Fassett wanted me to be exposed to all kinds of music, and around this time he took me to my first opera at the Met. It was *Götterdämmerung,* with Helen Traubel and Lauritz Melchior. I thought it would never end. Then he took me to *Pelléas et Mélisande,* with Bidù Sayão, Martial Singher, Ezio Pinza, and Margaret Harshaw. It was as thrilling as *Götterdämmerung* had been butt-numbing. Right then and there, I felt the sensual power of French music. Over the next several years, Jim Fassett programmed a lot of French works for me at CBS. Not too long after I saw *Pelléas,* I got to do the last act of Charpentier's *Louise,* with the great Singher himself. I could hardly believe it. I had never even heard of *Louise,* and here I was singing it with one of the greatest baritones in the world. I also sang "Il va venir" from Halévy's *La Juive,* "Plus de tourments" from Massenet's *Le cid,* Poulenc's "L'hôtel" and "Voyage à Paris," and many other French pieces.

I saw lots of musicals, too. My father had a first cousin in New York named Sadie Cullen, who ran a store that sold ladies' undergarments. Whenever she placed a big order, the top corset and lingerie salesmen would take her out to dinner and a show, and she'd ask me along as the extra girl. That's how I got to see *The Philadelphia Story* with Katharine Hepburn, *The Corn Is Green* with Ethel Barrymore, and *Bloomer Girl* with Celeste Holm—so many wonderful shows. I saw Helen Hayes in several plays, and even though she was the First Lady of the American Theater, I have to admit I never liked her acting. To me, it didn't matter what part she was playing, she was always Helen Hayes—just too perfect for words.

Now that I had my own show, I was earning decent money, seventy-eight dollars a week, and I could stop making all my own clothes. I still remember my first big purchase—a fox stole from Bonwit Teller. I thought, nothing but the best for me. Unfortunately, my *taste* wasn't the best. Not long ago, I came across a photo of me wearing that stole. I looked like a three-dollar whore.

Around this time, I met Al Stillman, who wrote the English lyrics to Ernesto Lecuona's lovely song "The Breeze and I." The tune hadn't really caught on big yet, and Al decided I would give it a great sales boost if I could get myself booked on the *Major Bowes Amateur Hour* and sing it. Now that I had my own show on the air, I couldn't get away with using my real name, because listeners would know I wasn't really an amateur, so I used my mother's name, Kitty Kennedy. I went over to Major Bowes's office on Broadway and sang "The Breeze and I."

"That's fine, Miss Kennedy," the major's people told me. "But the song's no good. What else do you have?"

"That's the only song I have."

They griped about it for a few minutes, then told me I was in. I went to the theater at the appointed hour and sang at the dress rehearsal. Out front, Major Bowes sat all by himself. He seemed like a sour old prune, and I sensed trouble right away. He didn't say a word after I finished, so I went backstage to sit with the other contestants and wait for showtime. Finally, one of the major's flunkies called me into a dressing room and told me I wouldn't be going on the air because the major didn't like my voice. So there I was, at age twenty-two, the star of my own show and a Major Bowes reject, all at once. "The Breeze and I," as it turned out, didn't need my help. It became one of the big hits of the 1940s.

Since my program aired at 11:30 at night, I assumed no one would hear it because most people would be asleep. But an amazing number of people *did* listen, and soon they began writing me fan letters. The show was popular enough to be picked up for another thirteen weeks, and then another. One night, after I sang some pop numbers on a broadcast, Harold Arlen called backstage to congratulate me. He asked me out to lunch, which was the beginning of a lifelong friendship. Peggy Wood, who later played *Mama* on TV, also phoned me one evening to tell me that my show was one of her favorites. Another night I was called to the telephone, and it was the Met soprano Helen Traubel, raving about my performance.

Things began to snowball. I was asked to make guest appearances on other radio programs, too. I performed often on André Kostelanetz's *The Pause That Refreshes.* "Kosty" was a marvelous singer's conductor. Sometimes his show would give a preview of songs from a Broadway musical that was about to open. I remember singing "Right as the Rain" from Harold Arlen's *Bloomer Girl.* I did lots of other programs, too—*Songs of the Centuries, The Prudential Family Hour, American Melody Hour,* and *County Castile* on WOR. One of CBS's most ambitious efforts was an hour-long program called *Invitation to Music.* Jim Fassett was the producer, but the real brains behind the show was Bernard Herrmann.

At the time, Benny was only in his midthirties, but he had already gotten off to a great start as a Hollywood film composer. He had written the music for Orson Welles's two great classics, *Citizen Kane* and *The Magnificent Ambersons,* and had won an Academy Award for his score of *The Devil and Daniel Webster,* starring Walter Huston and Edward Arnold. By the time I arrived at CBS, he had held various staff positions and now was chief conductor of the CBS Symphony.

Invitation to Music was Benny's pet project. He believed that radio music should challenge the audience, introducing them to unfamiliar works. I don't know about the audience, but many of the pieces he chose were unfamiliar to *me.* One day he came in with two selections from Alban Berg's *Wozzeck.* I'd never heard of twelve-tone music before, and I didn't know what to make of the pages Benny shoved in front of my face. But I went off to Charlie Baker, learned the music, and sang it on the air. It was tough, but a church picnic compared to what my future experience with *Wozzeck* would be. Another time, I sang Benny's own *Salammbô,* which had been used in *Citizen Kane.* Another favorite of those years was Charles Martin Loeffler's *Five Irish Fantasies.* I even sang the Liebestod from *Tristan und Isolde* and the

Immolation Scene from *Götterdämmerung*. Today, I can't imagine that any soprano in her early twenties would be allowed even to crack the spines on some of those scores. I didn't have a clue about what the words really meant; at that point, I'm sure the Liebestod was the only part of *Tristan* I bothered to learn. But Charlie Baker kept on drilling me, and I got through both pieces without getting fired.

Benny Herrmann craved recognition as a conductor, something that eluded him all his life. Eventually he was given a few chances to conduct the New York Philharmonic, but it never quite turned out the way he hoped it would. Mitch Miller remembers that Benny was kind of a virgin in the world of classical music. He'd be set to conduct a Haydn symphony on the air and have all the timings worked out carefully. Then he'd get all wrapped up in the andante section and drag it out so long that the orchestra would run out of time before it got to the final movement.

Maybe because he was insecure as a classical conductor, Benny's behavior was often a little on the erratic side. He'd be at the podium reviewing the score at around seven minutes to air time. The musicians would be arranging themselves in their seats. All of a sudden, Benny would start to twist his hair with one finger. Then he'd slam the score shut and shout, "To hell with all of you! I'm not going to conduct this!" and stomp out of the studio. We would all stand there, wondering how we were going to do the broadcast without a conductor. But every time, one of the guys would go after Benny and bring him back. Sometimes it might have been better if they hadn't found him. Benny didn't have what I would call great stick technique. It was a nightmare to try to follow him, especially when he pulled his favorite trick— conducting with one hand and picking his nose with the other.

One night I was in the studio and Benny came in, very excited, waving a score in one hand. "Eileen, I've got to play this for you!" I sat and listened as his hands flew over the keyboard, playing some of the most unusual music I'd ever heard. Every once in awhile, he'd sing out, "HEEEEEAAAATHCLIFF!" It turned out to be the opera he was working on, *Wuthering Heights.* It was marvelous, but unfortunately, Benny didn't live to see it performed onstage.

Eileen Farrell Sings was a sustaining (network-sponsored) program, which meant Jim Fassett had total freedom in programming it. But whenever I "guested" on a program with a major sponsor, like *The Prudential Family Hour,* there was a strict routine that had to be followed. The program aired on Sunday, so we rehearsed on Monday, Tuesday, and Wednesday. On Thursday there was a rehearsal with piano only, and a record would be made so the sponsors could listen to it before the Sunday broadcast and decide if there was anything that didn't meet with their approval. The baritone Earl Wrightson sang regularly on *The Prudential Family Hour,* and he was famous for his sewer mouth, as well as for being a big practical joker. One week, as the sponsor's record was being made, Earl took out a cigarette lighter and set fire to the bottom of the announcer's script. The poor guy had to keep reading faster and faster to get to the end before his copy went up in flames. He got through it so fast there would have been room for three times the number of commercials.

But if you really wanted to make trouble, you bided your time until the live broadcast. Once, on *Songs of the Centuries,* the guest was Emery Deutsch, who was known as the "Gypsy Violinist." Right before air time, the show's announcer usually went out and got loaded in one of the bars along Fifty-second Street. On this particular day, as Deutsch began to play, the announcer suddenly leaned down and began to roll up the violinist's left pant leg very slowly. When he had rolled it up to his knee, he started on the right pant leg. All the poor guy could do was stand there, getting madder and madder as he kept on playing, trying to shake down his pant legs. I was laughing so hard I had a handkerchief pressed over my mouth to muffle the sound, but it got through anyway, because when the broadcast was finished, Master Control telephoned downstairs and wanted to know what the hell had happened.

Working at CBS was one giant singing binge. I did everything—even pop songs from time to time. Many of the classically trained singers who worked a lot on radio—Risë Stevens, Dorothy Kirsten, and me, among others—didn't consider singing pop nearly as much of a leap as opera singers seem to today. Once I was asked to appear as a guest on *Your Hit Parade.* Jim Fassett didn't want me to do it because he thought it would somehow damage my reputation as the star of *Eileen Farrell Sings.* So I got him to agree to let me do it under a phony name. I chose "Dimples Lunsford." That may sound like a horse who came in third at Belmont, but it was Eileen Farrell and nobody else.

I worked like a fiend at CBS and loved every minute of it. Thanks to Charlie Baker, I was always so well prepared that I felt secure—not at all nervous. Only once do I remember making a fool of myself on the air. Margaret Harshaw and I were singing the Act 2 duet from *Aida,* and when I went for the high C, I cracked that son of a bitch wide open. When the orchestra stopped playing, Margaret turned and patted me on the shoulder. She had a funny expression on her face—whether it was sympathy or delight, I couldn't tell. Not that it really mattered. The great thing about having such a frantic radio schedule was that nothing seemed permanent. Once you were finished, it was on to the next thing. There was no time to worry about a cracked high C.

CHAPTER FOUR

NCE MY CAREER in radio got going, I was making too much money to keep on living at the Evangeline. I stayed for a while at the Wellington Hotel on Seventh Avenue. Then I found a furnished apartment, complete with a Steinway grand, at the Osborne on Fifty-seventh Street, diagonally across from Carnegie Hall. On December 7, 1941, I was standing on the corner of Fifty-seventh and Seventh, waiting to catch a bus so I could go down to Mass at Saint Patrick's Cathedral. As I got on board, I heard all the other passengers buzzing to each other. "Isn't it terrible?" said the woman next to me. "Pearl Harbor was bombed. We've declared war on Japan."

Even before we entered the war, my brother, John, had been drafted into the Army. He was still working for Towle up in Newburyport, Massachusetts, but now as a photographer, shooting advertisements for magazines such as *Harper's Bazaar* and *Vogue*. The Army assigned him to the aerial photography division in Denver. From there he went to officer's training at Yale University. (He and his wife, Sylvia, settled in New Haven, where their first child, Susan, was born.) Glenn Miller and his band were stationed there, too, and every day at lunch, they would play for the officers. Entertainers were expected to participate in the war effort, and I did my share, singing at the Stage Door Canteen in Manhattan. Once, while John was stationed at Yale, I took a train from Grand Central Station with Rose Marie, Zero Mostel, and a bunch of others to perform at a bond rally on the football field. When we got there, Glenn Miller and his band were being driven around the field in jeeps, playing "American Patrol" as the soldiers performed a marching drill.

John was transferred to Cape Cod for a final round of training, then assigned to duty in New Guinea. I went home to Woonsocket and drove up to Cape Cod with the rest of the family to see John off. He wrote often, but we never stopped worrying about him.

In 1944, I made a special Christmas recording that was going to be shipped overseas and played for the American boys on Christmas Eve. Shirley Temple was the mistress of ceremonies, and Jan Peerce and I sang a program of carols. By this time, John was stationed in Leyte, in the Philippines. One of his buddies heard that on Christmas night my record was going to be played on the radio. John went out looking for a shortwave set to see if he could pick it up. John told the rest of the story in a letter to me, which was published by *The New Yorker*.

One of the boys said we had a small station here, so I called them up. "Eileen Farrell?" he said. "My favorite singer. No, we have no records of her, but I'll call every station around."

Five minutes later, a fellow yelled, "Jack, your sister is singing on our station!" I rushed over, but a red alert cut the station off. I found out where the station was and blundered into the jungle to find it. Three of the station boys used to be on the production staff at CBS. The alert stopped as I got there, so they went back on the air. The announcer said, "The unusual is always happening. That talented young singer, Eileen Farrell, made a Christmas record for overseas a few months ago. Tonight, here in the studio, is her brother, Lieutenant Farrell, eagerly waiting to hear her voice." Then they played the record . . . I was thrilled to death.

When I graduated from high school at age nineteen, I still didn't know where babies came from. God knows, my mother never would have told me. So I learned about sex from listening to the other girls at the Evangeline. Most of the time, I was pretty confused. Once, after I had just moved to New York, I went out on a blind date with a fellow. When he took me home in a taxi, he kissed me goodnight. I didn't sleep all night—I just *knew* I was going to have a baby.

I hadn't had a steady boyfriend since my junior year in high school, when I started going out with Charlie Dubuque. Charlie was a year younger than I was—a tall, skinny, good-looking boy who used to take me walking on Saturday nights. One Saturday, Charlie came by as usual, and my father entertained him in the living room while I was upstairs fixing my hair. For some reason, my father thought it would be funny to tell Charlie that next year I was going to start studying the tuba. I doubt if poor Charlie even knew what a tuba was, but he liked me very much. The next thing I knew, he had signed up for marching band and was weaving all over the field trying to hang onto that tuba.

Charlie Dubuque grew up to become a policeman. I must have had an eye for them, even then.

By 1942, *Eileen Farrell Sings* was going strong on CBS. Once in a while, one of the thirteen-week segments would be moved to a different time slot, but the audience always seemed to follow. (In the years to come, they'd go back and forth with the title, and sometimes it was called *Eileen Farrell Presents*.)

It was a wonderful time in my life. I still didn't have any particular burning career ambitions. I was just happy to be singing, and I tackled everything that Jimmie Fassett threw at me. Sometimes, when I went for a coaching, Charlie Baker would open the music and say, "Jeeeeesus! They want you to learn this? This is *hard!*" I never looked at it that way. I had a job to do, and I did it.

It's probably just as well that I had this attitude, because I was thrown into some pretty heady company in those early days. Once, Erich Wolfgang Korngold came to the studio to conduct me in an evening of his music. He had been living in the U.S. for some time, writing film scores for Warner Brothers, out in Hollywood. I sang Marietta's Lied from his opera *Die Tote Stadt,* and several other songs and arias. I still have the scores I sang from that evening, with Korngold's markings where he changed certain words and notes that I was having trouble with.

I also sang occasionally with Frank Sinatra. The shows I did with him didn't have an audience, so we didn't have to sing over the screaming bobby-soxers who trailed after him everywhere. Once, a guest who was going to appear on Frank's show canceled at the last minute, and I filled in for her. Frank and I sang "People Will Say We're in Love." Luckily, I still have a tape of it.

After a while, Jimmie Fassett decided I should sing for the great German soprano Lotte Lehmann. Jimmie idolized Lehmann, and since he knew her slightly, he wanted to show off his new discovery. Along with Vera Brodsky, a pianist on the CBS music staff, Jimmie and I went up to see Mme. Lehmann at her apartment near Carnegie Hall.

There I was, about to sing for one of the greatest German lieder singers of all time. So why did I choose to do Brahms songs? I mean, when I tell you I'm stupid, you've got to believe me. On top of that, Lehmann was famous for being tough on

young students, especially women. I sang two or three of the
Brahms songs, and they seemed to go well. I looked at Vera; she
was beaming. I looked at Jim; *he* was beaming. Then I looked
over at Mme. Lehmann. She was not beaming. She had been re-
clining on a sofa the whole time I'd been singing and hadn't
budged an inch. There was a beautifully timed pause. Then she
said, "Vell . . . I tell you. I suggest you go home . . . and have lots
of babies."

Poor Jimmie looked as if he were going to cry. We thanked
Lehmann for her time. On the ride down in the elevator, no one
said a word. When we got out onto Fifty-seventh Street, Jimmie
blew up. "You sang so beautifully! How dare she say a thing like
that?" We walked around the block until he calmed down. I
couldn't understand why he was so upset. I was almost embarrassed to tell him it hadn't bothered me in the least.

It seemed like every week, I met another fascinating person.
One day, as I was having coffee in Colbee's, Mitch Miller came
in with a sort of rumpled-looking man wearing a tweed jacket
and gray flannels. His name was Alec Wilder. I had never heard
of him. "Alec is a terrific composer," said Mitch. "You'll love his
songs." Mitch was right. Before long, I was singing a whole
group of Alec's songs on my weekly program. His most famous
one was a lovely, sad number, "I'll Be Around." Lots of people
sang it, but the Mills Brothers are the ones who really made it
click in the 1940s.

Alec was never interested in pleasing the public. His melodies didn't stay in your head as easily as, say, Rodgers and Hart's
or Harold Arlen's. The charm of Alec's tunes didn't exactly leap to
the surface—you had to listen to them a few times before you really began to get a grasp on them. But he certainly knew how to
write for the voice. One of my favorites was "It's So Peaceful in
the Country," which he composed for Mildred Bailey in the '40s.
He also wrote wonderful instrumental music for unusual en-

sembles. One of his favorite combinations was harpsichord and wind instruments, and he formed a group, the Alec Wilder Octet, to play these pieces. (Mitch Miller was the oboist.)

Like Benny Herrmann, Alec was an extremely complicated man who seemed to make a hobby of irritating people. He was very well-bred, and yet he could be absolutely foul mouthed when he was mad about something. Off and on throughout his life, he was a heavy drinker. He was downright rude if he didn't think you belonged. Generally speaking, he didn't care for women at all. Alec wrote a number of songs with Loonis Mc-Glohon, the talented composer/lyricist/jazz pianist. Once, when they were working on something together, Alec went to stay with Loonis and his wife, Nan, at their home in Charlotte, North Carolina. During the whole time Alec was there, Nan made his bed and cooked his meals, but Alec wouldn't say a word to her. He didn't acknowledge her presence in any way. After he left, Nan cornered Loonis and said, "I want you to speak with him. If he's ever going to come back here, he can't treat me that way." Poor Alec lived so totally in his own world that he wasn't even aware of what he'd done.

Alec spared no one. Once he heard Peggy Lee perform one of his songs. Alec hated to have his music tampered with, and Peggy had changed something in the bridge. Alec confronted her and demanded to know why she'd made the change.

"But Alec," Peggy said, "I needed to do it to get through the bridge."

"Peggy," said Alec, "do me a favor. The next time you do one of my songs, when you get to the bridge, jump."

For some reason, Alec never turned on me, and we became the best of friends. He even composed a song cycle, *Songs for Patricia*, when my daughter Kathleen was born in 1953. The title confused me; I guess he was hoping I would name her Patricia, but I never asked him about it. I'm thankful I never saw his dark side. I only remember his fatherly concern for me, his raspy voice, his rich, buffo laugh, and his beautiful music.

Since I was gradually making bigger money, I could afford to spruce up my wardrobe a little, and I decided to have some first-class clothes made by one of the New York specialists. One night after a broadcast, I had gotten a call from a couturier named Herman Patrick Tappé, who ran a salon, the House of Tappé, at 25 West Fifty-seventh Street. Herman was a tall, handsome, white-haired fellow who claimed, despite the manufactured last name, to be a real Irishman. He did it all—dresses, hats, furs, coats—the works. When he called, he told me how much he loved my program and how much he would love to make some clothes for me. So I made an appointment to see him. We hit it off, and he wound up designing several stunning outfits for me.

A short while later, Herman ran into some trouble. Someone had forged his name on a $10,000 check, and he had called in the police. The man on the NYPD forgery squad assigned to handle Herman's case was Robert Vincent Reagan. One of the first things Officer Reagan did was take a look at Herman's list of clients. When he came to my name, he said, "Oh—I listen to her on the radio every week." Herman saw a chance to do some matchmaking. "Well, her name is Farrell and yours is Reagan," he said. "You're a nice Irishman, and she's a nice Irish girl. Why don't the two of you come out some time and have lunch with me?" Bob was agreeable, so Herman called me, and we made a lunch date.

The three of us went to the Gripsholm, a wonderful Scandinavian restaurant on East Fifty-seventh Street. I sized up Bob Reagan right away. He was a tall man with a nose that had been broken several times. He was immaculately dressed. I've always made a point of noticing men's shoes; Bob's were so polished they shone, and his heels weren't worn down. He had beautiful, old-fashioned manners. When we met, he bowed as he shook my hand. When we sat down, he took my napkin off the table and put it in my lap. No one had ever done that for me before. Things were off to a good start.

We had a lovely lunch. Afterward, I was on my way to see *The Corn Is Green* on Broadway. He dropped me off at the theater, and as we were saying good-bye he asked if he could take me to dinner on the following Sunday. I told him that I was doing *The Pause That Refreshes,* but that I'd be happy to go out with him afterward. I asked him if he'd like to come to the show. The following Sunday, he came to the broadcast at Liederkranz Hall, and then we went for dinner at the Lobster, in the west forties. I ordered a delicious steamed lobster, and after I had demolished it, Bob asked me if I would like dessert.

"Actually," I said, "I'd like another lobster."

So he ordered one for me. All in all, a terrific first date.

Over the next few weeks, we saw more and more of each other. Bob was always so courtly. Once, we were in a nightclub, and two men at the next table, who had put away several rounds of drinks, started using some pretty raw language. They got louder and louder, and soon Bob leaned over and said, "Pardon me. Would you mind not using that kind of language in front of Miss Farrell?" Now, I'm sure these two fellows didn't have a clue about who "Miss Farrell" was. But to Bob Reagan, I was obviously a somebody. They took one look at him, probably figured he had a broken nose for a good reason, and didn't say a word for the rest of the evening. Here I was, accustomed to spending all my time with the guys in the orchestra at CBS; with their sweat-stained shirts and cigars, they looked like a bunch of thugs. I wasn't used to being treated like an Irish princess, but I was starting to think that maybe I could learn.

Ever since I had come to New York, I had put myself completely in the hands of other people. In the case of Jim Fassett and Charlie Baker, it couldn't have worked out better. Jim continued to choose the music for my show, constantly opening my eyes to new and unusual repertory, and off I would go to polish it at Charlie's studio in the Ansonia. Merle Alcock was another story. Even though I was aware that she wasn't teaching me much of anything I didn't already know—we didn't really touch on technique at all—I didn't know what to do about it.

In a very short time, Bob Reagan told me *just* what to do about it. Bob was a smart businessman all his life, and he pointed out that it was ridiculous for me to give Merle 10 percent of my earnings. He explained to me that in spite of her suggestion that I audition for CBS, she couldn't lay any real claim to my success. As a teacher, she wasn't helping me either: Hadn't I told him time and time again that I wasn't learning anything, that I was just treading water? Bob encouraged me to tell Merle that I was leaving her and that our contractual agreement was finished.

"I can't do that," I said. "I'd be too scared to tell her that."

"So write her a letter," he said.

"I can't! What if I ran into her on the street?"

"You can't live your life that way. What she's doing isn't right."

Bob wouldn't let up, and eventually, I sat down and wrote a letter to Merle Alcock. I thanked her for everything she had done for me, and told her I had decided to stop studying for a while. I said that since we wouldn't be working together any longer, I considered our financial agreement to be void.

And the funny thing is, I never heard a word from her. Some time later, as I feared, I did run into her, on West Fifty-seventh Street. I was so nervous I could hardly speak, but she couldn't have been nicer, and she made no mention at all of the letter. I never saw her again. I think that if Bob hadn't been in the picture, Merle might have put up a fight, and even taken me to court. But even she knew enough not to argue with a cop.

Still, this left me without a teacher. A friend in the CBS chorus recommended a man who happened to be in Merle's building. When I went to him for my first lesson, he explained his theory of singing. He pointed to my neck and said that there was a hole inside, and the voice had to be directed out through that hole. I thought this sounded very strange, but I gave it a try. After two weeks, I couldn't sing above an A, so that was the end of that. One day in 1944, during a coaching session at the Ansonia with Charlie Baker, I mentioned that I was on the lookout for a new teacher. Charlie told me there was someone right in the building who might be perfect for me. Her name was Eleanor McLellan.

Charlie made a phone call, and within a week I was in Miss McLellan's studio, having my first lesson. Miss "Mac" had a dark, high-ceilinged apartment that went on forever on the eighteenth floor of the Ansonia. In the living room was a magnificent Steinway grand, almost buried from sight because of all the music stacked on it. Music also covered every other available surface in the living room, and the dining room, too.

Miss Mac was a large, white-haired Southern woman with an enormous bosom that hit her somewhere around the small intestine. When I met her, she must have been in her midsixties. For teaching, she always wore either an old-fashioned floral print dress or a sensible suit. She was always carefully made up and wore a pince-nez. She commanded everything and everyone in her path, including her husband, Walter Kiesewetter, also a voice teacher. He had an enormous pile of white hair that went straight up, sort of like the father of the Katzenjammer Kids in the comics. Miss Mac liked to tell a story about an evening when she and her husband attended a concert at Carnegie Hall. She was wearing a very elaborate hat, which was blocking the view of the man behind her. When he asked her to remove it, she refused and offered to change places with her husband instead. This didn't help matters any, because Mr. Kiesewetter's hair shot up even higher than Miss Mac's hat!

Miss Mac had been teaching for years. In addition to having been a fine singer herself, she was also an accomplished pianist, harpist, and violinist. I seem to recall that she was some shirttail relation to the great American diva Lillian Nordica. Later, I found out that she thought I had the stuff that the great divas of Nordica's day were made of. At the time, however, she gave no indication that she was impressed by me in the least. At that first lesson, she sat down at the piano, and we went through a few things. When I was finished, she leaned back and said matter-of-factly, "Very good. But we have lots of work to do."

Did we ever. I started going to Miss Mac three times a week, a schedule I would maintain, whenever I was in town, for more than fifteen years. Miss Mac redirected me as a singer. The first thing she told me was that I didn't have the remotest idea of how to breathe properly. "Sing on the breath," she would say. "You don't take a breath, wait for a beat or two and then start to sing. It's all one continuous movement, whether it's slow or fast. You inhale and then begin to sing as you exhale."

Miss Mac also taught me the secret of solid breath support. She stopped me from breathing from my upper chest, as I had been doing for years. Breathing from the upper chest tends to create tension in the neck and throat muscles. Miss Mac explained that proper breath support originates from the diaphragm. When your doctor examines your lungs with a stethoscope, he listens over your chest, but also over your back, extending almost halfway down to your waist. All of that space contains lung—to breathe and move air. Many people might think that the diaphragm simply separates the lungs from the rest of the body, but it's almost all muscle, and it gives you about 85 percent of your breathing capacity.

Breathing from the diaphragm sounds easy, but it was foreign to me at the time, and tough to master. If I was giving a recital, I would try to apply what Miss Mac had taught me for the first group of songs. I'd be OK for a while, and then I would start to lose control of my voice. I'd think, my God, if I keep this up, I'll never make it to the end of the program—and before the night was out, I'd revert to my old way of breathing. But I kept working at it, and gradually it got easier. Miss Mac showed me how to develop my breath control with a simple exercise I could do as I walked down the street. All you do is breathe in rhythm as you walk: inhale, one step, two steps, three steps, four steps; exhale, one step, two steps, three steps, four steps. It took close to two years to absorb Miss Mac's breathing techniques, but it was worth the wait. Learning to control my breathing was the greatest power trip I'd ever known. Once I had that control, I had the security to tackle just about anything within my range. Today I see so many young singers with big international careers who don't have the faintest idea about basic breath support. Without it, their singing years are going to be cut short.

Miss Mac taught me another lesson that remained with me for my entire career: Don't listen to yourself. She explained that if I sang in her studio, then went down to the stage of Carnegie Hall and sang there, it would sound different in each space. Therefore, I would be trying to adjust my voice for every space in which I sang—a surefire way of getting yourself into serious vocal trouble. "Don't go by the way it sounds," Miss Mac warned me. "Go by the way it feels inside." I had natural forward placement of my voice to begin with, and Miss Mac taught me to focus it even more. She stressed perfect diction. Over and over she would have me repeat, "The lips, the teeth, the tip of the tongue."

Miss Mac taught me to sing as I spoke. When you sing a lyric, you should go immediately for the vowel, but that doesn't mean you distort it. Just sing it naturally, as you would say it. Take any old pop song—"I Only Have Eyes for You" will do. Try speaking the first line, "Are there stars out tonight?" When you speak it, you don't drop your jaw on the word "stars." So why do it when you sing "stars"? Yet many singers don't understand this, and make it twice as hard as is necessary. When Jessye Norman sings a simple hymn like "Balm in Gilead," she tears into the word "Baaaaaaaaaalm" as if she's doing facial aerobics.

When I went to Miss Mac, I had trouble singing pianissimo, and we spent months working on that until I could manage it with ease. She also helped me extend my upper register. "If you're going to sing a good high C," she'd say, "You've got to vocalize at least one or two notes above it." One of the more controversial things she told me was that I shouldn't think about the break in the voice. "There is no such thing," she'd snap. Teachers are always getting students psyched out about how to negotiate the break, and the result is that lots of singers become so terrified that they wind up really grinding their gears. Often they wind up with three entirely different sounds in their top, middle, and lower registers. Some people who went on to become big stars still sing that way. It sounds awful, and I can't understand why teachers permit it. When I was young, Gladys Swarthout was one of the most popular mezzos around, but she had the worst break I ever heard in my life. We used to call her Gladys Sorethroat. As I moved into the upper register, she taught me how to "feel" as if I were actually singing lower, and vice-versa. This comes from full breath support and control. It's a good method of developing an even quality throughout your entire range. (Of course, your highest notes will resonate in your head in a very different way from your low notes—mine used to go out the back of my head.)

The single most important thing Miss Mac taught me may have been to get across the meaning of the words. This is something else that so many young singers today don't seem to appreciate. They may be note-perfect, but they don't pay attention to the words. The words are *so* important. Week in and week out, Miss Mac taught me how to tell a story in song, how to color the words and bring out their meaning to make music come to life.

In all the years I studied with Miss Mac, she never took one cent from me. "You can't imagine how many pupils have come through the door since word got out that you've been studying with me," she'd say. "I couldn't possibly take any money from you." She gave free lessons to many of her students. There was one young mezzo who became her secretary as a way of paying for her lessons. She was there every week when I went for mine, ushering students into the foyer. She lived with her sister, and just the way she would say, in her reedy little voice, "Sister and I went to the movies last night" would make you laugh. Her name was Alice Ghostley.

Each week, I could hardly wait to get to the Ansonia for my lessons with Miss Mac. She was strict with me, but she was also warm and nurturing in a way that Merle Alcock never had been. Miss Mac's methods were practical and sensible. I don't recall that we ever talked about the positioning of the pharynx, the larynx, or any of the other things so many teachers go on and on about. I've heard about teachers who make their students lie down on the floor! I would love to know what Miss Mac would have had to say about this kind of nonsense.

It wasn't long after I started seeing Bob Reagan that I knew I was really in love. In many ways, he was a typical, tough New York cop. He was stubborn, and he had a temper that could flare up without much warning. But he had a gentler side, too. Bob loved to read, especially history and political biographies and autobiographies. He loved music, too—mostly popular music, although he did enjoy opera. Bob had a fine tenor voice and sang in the Police Glee Club. (You could really tell Bob was a tenor when he got mad about something; his voice would sail up into the stratosphere.) His favorite song was "Falling in Love with Love." He loved the melody and didn't think much about the words. And he tried hard to convince me that it was "our" song. He didn't like it when I pointed out that the lyrics—"Falling in love with love is falling for make believe/Falling in love with love is playing the fool"—are really very sad.

After Bob and I had been seeing each other for several months, my parents were naturally curious to meet him. One weekend, I took him home to Woonsocket with me. Everything went smoothly enough on this first meeting. From the start, Bob and my father liked each other enormously. My mother was another story. On the surface, she was always polite to Bob, but I could tell right away that she didn't like the idea of anyone getting serious about her little girl. Her reaction didn't have anything to do with Bob's personality, although he and my mother definitely were not meant to be soul mates. She wouldn't have liked any man who came into my life. Like a lot of mothers, she believed nobody was good enough for her daughter.

But I was a goner for Bob, and after a while, it started to bother me that we didn't seem to be moving any closer to marriage. This was the 1940s, of course, and women didn't propose. I waited and waited for a proposal. No luck. One day, when I was at CBS, rehearsing my show, I started to sing something and suddenly burst into tears. Julie Baker, Bernie Greenhouse, and the other guys in the orchestra just sat there and dropped their eyes to the floor, not knowing what to do. I was so upset I did something I'd never done before and haven't done since: I picked up my music and walked out. As I was waiting for the elevator, Mitch Miller came running after me and asked me what was wrong. I poured out the whole story to him, and I'll never forget the pep talk he gave me. "You've got a great career going," he said. "You can't let yourself get all upset over a thing like this. If you and Bob are meant to get married, it will happen. Just be patient and keep your mind on your work." Good old Mitch. I walked out of the CBS building and all the way home. That was probably the longest walk of my life. At the time, I didn't give a damn about being a famous singer. I just wanted to be Mrs. Robert Reagan.

CHAPTER FIVE

I DON'T REMEMBER much about the sacrifices we had to make at home during the war years, so they can't have been all that bad. Tucked away in an old cookbook, I still have a recipe in my mother's handwriting for something called "War Cake": It's filled with raisins and nuts, and molasses instead of sugar. Through some of his connections, Bob Reagan kept me stocked with nylons, so no hardship there.

Mostly what I remember about the war years is how busy I was on the radio. I did my own program all season long, and when it went on hiatus, I did *The Prudential Family Hour*. I also sang on a weekday program sponsored by Libbey Owens Illinois Glass, and during one thirteen-week segment, I developed a throat ailment and was replaced by the wonderful soprano Dorothy Kirsten. Dorothy was a close friend of mine, and one of the few opera singers who were good pop stylists, too; she got quite a following singing with Frank Sinatra on *Light Up Time*. The money for the Libbey Owens show was terrific, and she used it to buy herself a Steinway grand. She was so grateful, she named it "Eileen Farrell."

Once, I even sang on a dramatic program that starred Mercedes McCambridge and James Mason. Miss McCambridge played a singer, and I did the vocals. Afterward, Mr. Mason came up to me and said, "I want you to sing that at my funeral." I got to be such a well-known name on radio that I even made it into the lyrics of a Cole Porter song, "Big Town," which he wrote for a show called *Seven Lively Arts* (1944). An aspiring singer sings about her hopes for a career behind the mike:

> If Ginny Simms and Georgia Carroll
> and Dinah Shore and Eileen Farrell
> and Mildred Bailey
> Can night and daily
> impress the public so
> Then I too can wa-hoo
> and sing on the radio!

Even with this kind of attention, I never had a chance to get a swelled head, because Miss Mac kept me in constant check. Under her training, the top of my voice had developed quite a bit. But Miss Mac never stopped cracking the whip. Often after a radio broadcast, she would say, "I hope you didn't think you did well last night." Well . . . sometimes I *did*.

For some time, my mother had been making noises about wanting to move to New York. In the midforties she and my father left Woonsocket and joined me in a rented house on Staten Island. But the daily commute wore me down after a while, so I rented a spectacular fourteen-room apartment at the Apthorp on Seventy-ninth and Broadway, and invited my parents and Leona to come and live with me. There was plenty of room—in fact, when my brother, John, got back from overseas, he and his wife, Sylvia, and their family eventually moved in with us, too.

One of the great things New York had to offer in those years was the night life—Café Society Uptown, Le Ruban Bleu, the Blue Angel, and the Byline Room, for example. Fifty-second Street was hopping with all kinds of clubs—the Red Door, the Onyx Club, and lots of others, all of them long gone now. But the place I remember best of all is Tony's West Side. It was on Fifty-second Street off Sixth Avenue, and the reason it was so important to me was that Mabel Mercer played there.

Mabel was born in Burton-on-Trent, England. Her father was black and her mother was white. Her father ran off, and her mother dumped her with relatives when she was still a little girl. She was mostly brought up by the nuns at her convent school. Mabel spent a little time in vaudeville, but she really made a name for herself playing at Bricktop, the well-known Paris nightclub. That was where she developed her famous style. At Bricktop, customers would often ask her to come over to their table and sing a song. She found she couldn't sing directly to them because it made them self-conscious. So she came up with a way of *not* looking at them as she sang, and of using the lyrics to tell a story so that they would concentrate on the song instead of on her, almost as if they were watching a play.

When the war heated up, Mabel's timing was bad: She was away in the Bahamas doing a singing engagement, and for a while she was stranded there. But she wanted to get to the States, so she married an American jazz musician just to get U.S. citizenship. Soon after she landed in New York, she sang an engagement at Tony's West Side. It was so successful that Tony's became her home base for the rest of the 1940s. When I first heard Mabel there, around 1942, she still had a good mezzo voice. Over time, her voice started to go downhill, but she never lost any of her ability to phrase, to create a mood, to get across the power of the words. It was almost like listening to Katharine Cornell if Katharine Cornell had been able to sing. Lots of composers said they'd rather hear her sing their songs than anybody else. She was so mesmerizing that you forgave her for not making pretty sounds. (Today, I notice that so many young singers, both in opera and pop, seem to have the opposite problem: They're so busy concentrating on their pear-shaped tones that they forget about the words altogether.)

Mabel caught on in a big way at Tony's and the other Manhattan clubs where she played. It usually took people some time to get her message, but if they came back to hear her a couple of times, they couldn't help getting it. One evening, shortly after I had met Bob Reagan, I asked him to come with me to hear Mabel sing. I was very nervous that he might think she was just too offbeat and hate every minute of it. But he fell in love with her from the get-go. Another time, I took my friend Kitty Morris to hear Mabel sing at Tony's. Kitty liked to drink, and she'd tossed back quite a few by the time Mabel came out to sing her first number. Mabel had gotten only a few bars into her song when Kitty turned to me and said, right out loud, "JEEEEEESUS! SHE CAN'T SING!" I managed to quiet her down for awhile, but she kept ordering round after round, and every now and then, she'd tune up again: "OH, SHIT! SHE CAN'T SING AT ALL!" I don't know how I managed to sit through that performance, but Mabel wasn't fazed by it at all. By that point in her career, she was probably used to dealing with saloon crowds.

One of Mabel's biggest fans was Frank Sinatra, and he was also very much influenced by her. The big-band sound had been going strong for years, and up until the middle of the forties, most pop singers took their cue from the big-band soloists. The melody was everything, and what you aimed for was smooth, even-keel vocalism. You didn't fool around much with the phrases, or hold onto a word for emphasis, or pause for dramatic effect. But then all that started to change. More and more night-clubs were popping up, and they demanded a more intimate style of performing. Listen to recordings of singers like Margaret Whiting, Rosemary Clooney, and Peggy Lee from the forties. Then listen to their later work, after they had found their own personal voices and styles, and you'll hear a huge difference.

I became a Mabel Mercer groupie. Cy Walter accompanied her at the piano and Mabel would sit in a straight-backed chair, wearing a simple black dress with a beautiful stole—her clothes were always very simple but very elegant. She made me listen to Rodgers and Hart's "Little Girl Blue" or Cole Porter's "It's Delovely" as if I were hearing it for the first time. Mabel was one of the classiest ladies I've ever known, but she was no prude. I can still see how her eyes would light up right before she was about to launch into some slightly racy lyric.

One funny thing about Mabel—even though she was citified in so many ways and loved New York nightlife, she was most at home in her farm up in East Chatham, New York, working in her garden and canning batches of jam, jelly, and applesauce. She was crazy about animals, and if a squirrel or a bird broke its leg, she would bring it into the house and try to put a splint on it. From time to time, when the music business got to be too much for him, Alec Wilder used to take rest cures up at Mabel's farm. Mabel had a special room where Alec stayed, and when she found out how much he loved walnut trees, she planted one just outside the window. (Actually, it turned out to be a hickory, but I don't think she ever told him, and I don't think Alec ever noticed the difference.)

The only down side of going to Tony's to listen to Mabel was Tony Soma himself. He was a frustrated opera singer, and a real slob. Before Mabel came out, Tony would walk up one side of the room and then the other, shaking hands with everyone and telling them all how good it was to see them. Then he would go up by the piano and stand on his head and sing opera arias in a real Italian peasant's voice. This would go on for maybe twenty minutes or so, and then his children would go from table to table collecting money. It was awful, but at least he was smart enough to realize he had a gold mine in Mabel.

Mabel and I became fast friends. I talked to her a lot about how she developed her style, and before long, I had completely rethought the way I sang pop songs. On my own, I started to fool around with the words and phrases, trying to make the songs tell a story as they did when Mabel sang them. I had one that was a special favorite—Rodgers and Hart's "He Was Too Good to Me." I first heard Lulu Jean Norman sing it at a party, accompanied by Bobby Tucker. I was knocked out by what Lulie did with that song, and I decided to go to work on it myself.

By this time, I was part of a crowd of musicians who got together at each other's apartments for evenings of partying and music. It was quite a group—Mabel and Cy Walter, Fritz Steinway, Carol Glenn and her husband, Eugene List, Dorothy Kirsten, and a wonderful young mezzo named Christine Johnson. Christine was singing small parts at the Met and not getting much of anywhere, but one night at a New Year's Eve party at Carol and Eugene's apartment, Dick Rodgers heard Christine sing. He signed her right up to play Nettie Fowler in *Carousel* on Broadway. I would get up at those parties and sing "He Was Too Good to Me," and everybody loved it. I so enjoyed this music, and I hoped I might get a chance to do more of it professionally.

Singing on the radio during the war years, I often felt that I was brought close to all the big events of the day as they happened. We were always being called in to sing for some important occasion or to mark somebody's passing. I especially remember singing after Franklin Delano Roosevelt died in April 1945. CBS stopped all its regular broadcasts for a couple of days and programmed nonstop music. Everybody under contract was called in to perform. After a while, all the seriousness got to me. Several times, Sandy Becker, one of CBS's announcers, and I slipped out of the building to go for a walk up to the Central Park Zoo off Fifth Avenue. The weather was warm, all the trees were in bloom, and we just walked along without saying much. It was hard for us to believe that the President was gone. The following year, I performed *The Last Speech*, Roosevelt's final written words set to music by Lou Cooper.

I made some wonderful, lasting friendships during the radio years—none more important than with Shirley Cowell. We met while I was working on *The Prudential Family Hour*. She was friendly with one of the producers and came with him to a rehearsal one afternoon. She had just graduated from a finishing school, and she had lovely manners. I never heard her swear—the worst she'd say was, "Well, cow's ankles!" But she was also very funny, and she'd crack one joke after another in her gravelly smoker's voice. We hit it off immediately.

Shirley was a midwestern girl, born to money, who loved show business and wanted to be part of it. She came from a musical family—her grandmother had graduated from the Peabody Institute—but Shirley couldn't read music. Eventually she had her own radio program down in Florida, where she moved because of her severe asthma. While she was there, she managed to lick a serious drinking problem she'd been battling for years. And the thing that really speeded her recovery was songwriting. While she was in her drying-out phase, she would take a tape recorder and thesaurus and go sit beside her swimming pool. She would sing a melody into the tape recorder and write out the lyrics. Then she would send the tape to a friend, who would transcribe the tune onto staff paper. Some top singers, Johnny Mathis for one, eventually recorded some of her songs, and I put several of them, including "Here" and "Wasn't It a Lovely Evening?," on a compact disk myself. We remained the best of friends until her death in 1997. How we all miss her.

Shirley lived in Miami Beach for most of the year, but we used to get together whenever we could. I went down to Florida to visit her at least once a year, and there's one visit that sticks out in my mind. When I was in Miami Beach, Shirley and I often got together with Pansy Schenck. Pansy's husband, Joe, was the big movie executive who had once been chairman of the board of Twentieth Century–Fox. Their daughter, Marti Stevens, was a singer who was starting to get some attention for herself. One winter I had gone down to spend time with Shirley, and Pansy happened to call to ask us if we'd like to go with her to see Marlene Dietrich's act at the swanky club Fontainebleau. We said yes, of course, so Pansy sent her chauffeur for us and we met her at Fontainebleau. Now, I don't think Pansy had much of a clue about what any of her children were up to, but I thought she must have heard the rumors that Marti was having an affair with Marlene Dietrich, because it was fairly common gossip in show business circles.

We went to Marlene's show, and even though she couldn't sing worth a damn, she was absolutely fabulous. Burt Bacharach was her music director. I had met both Marlene and Burt when I had been doing the Casals Festival down in Puerto Rico several years earlier. Pansy had made arrangements for all of us to go backstage to visit Marlene, and when we got to her dressing room, she greeted me and said, "Oh, it's good to see you again." We chatted a bit, and then Pansy introduced herself.

"Hello," she said, "I'm Mrs. Joe Schenck. I think you know my daughter, Marti."

There was a perfectly timed pause. Then Marlene said with a knowing smile, "Oh, yes. I *do*."

Shirley and I wanted to die right then and there. Pansy just kept chattering away, and I don't think she ever figured out why Shirley and I were so tongue-tied.

I had almost given up hope that Bob Reagan would ever ask me to marry him, but he finally came through, and we were married April 5, 1946, in Yonkers, New York. We didn't have a honeymoon, since I had to report to CBS for a 10 a.m. rehearsal the following day. Bob had been married once before, to a model, but it hadn't lasted a year, and by the time I met him, it had been over for almost a decade. Both Bob and his first wife had been raised Catholic, and to get a divorce would have meant excommunication. So they got an annulment, but it was given by the state of New York, not the Catholic Church, which meant that in the Church's view, Bob was damaged goods. No church wedding for the Reagans.

My father liked Bob a lot, and I don't think he was bothered in the least by any of this. But my mother was *not pleased*. She didn't say much about it, but her silence was deafening. In truth, Bob's first marriage was just a convenient excuse. She didn't approve of Bob Reagan, and I'm afraid Bob didn't do much to get on her good side. For years after we were married, my mother would visit us for a week or so at a time. She and I would be sitting in the living room talking, and the minute Bob walked into the room, she would clam up. It used to infuriate him, and I used to plead with her not to do it, but she kept right on. The tension between them made me very uncomfortable, but there wasn't much I could do about it. They just weren't meant to get along.

Living with my parents was out of the question, so the Farrells packed up and returned to Woonsocket, and Bob and I moved into a one-room apartment on Staten Island. We weren't there very long before we bought a little Swiss-style white stucco house with red shutters, also on Staten Island. Shortly after our marriage I got pregnant. The baby was due in February 1947. I worked at my usual pace that season. I did my last radio show just before Christmas, then went on maternity leave. After the last broadcast, several of the guys in the orchestra came up to wish me luck. One was Julius Baker.

"Hey, Eileen, where are you going?"

There I stood, in a maternity dress that already managed to feel tight.

"What do you mean, where am I going, Julie? I'm going to have a baby."

"You're *kidding*. I didn't know that!"

Toward the end of 1946 I had begun having terrible pains in my back. I went to the doctor, who informed me that I had an ovarian cyst and would require surgery before I gave birth. It was a risky operation, and I was terrified that the baby and I might not make it. My mother came down from Woonsocket and was staying in the house with Bob. That terrified me almost as much. In the end, the cyst turned out to be the size of a large grapefruit, but the surgeons were able to remove both the right ovary and tube without harming the baby. My recovery was slow but steady, and I was happy that motherhood hadn't been dead-ended for me, since you can have as many babies as you want with a single ovary.

The week I was supposed to deliver, a terrible blizzard hit New York. The snow plow couldn't make it up the steep hill that our house was on. I looked out the front door, wondering if I was going to have the baby at home, laid out on my bed and biting on a wooden spoon.

"Don't worry," said Bob. Before long, a friend with a snow blower showed up and managed to get one lane clear. At six o'clock the next morning, I was on my way to the hospital. It was bitterly cold, but the sky was a gorgeous gray-blue, and the sunrise was so spectacular, I almost forgot about my contractions

With Robbie on his first day
of school. Personal collection of
Eileen Farrell.

for a few minutes. On February 25, 1947, Robert Vincent Reagan, Jr., was born. I thought he was the most beautiful child I'd ever seen. Bob was thrilled. He'd always longed to be a father, and one of the reasons he and his first wife split up was that she didn't want children.

I was wildly in love with my husband. We had a wonderful, healthy son. I was happily recuperating and looked forward to returning to work in a few months. Life was good.

CHAPTER SIX

Y 1947, THE END was in sight for the great days of radio. I had learned an enormous amount of music during my seven years at CBS, and eventually I started to repeat a lot of it. I lost count on "Dich, teure Halle" from *Tannhäuser* and Elsa's Traum from *Lohengrin*. I sang "Lover, Come Back to Me" so often that Julie Baker, Bernard Greenhouse, and the other guys in the orchestra would yell, "Oh, God! Not 'Lover, Back Up to Me' again!" The orchestra players were being snapped up by the TV industry, where the money was better. (By 1951, the CBS Symphony would disband once and for all.) I had no complaints. I'd had a terrific time and a good, long run. Now it was time to move on. So, around the time that Robbie was born, *Eileen Farrell Sings* signed off.

I was fairly heavy at the time, and nobody thought I had much of a future in television, so the next logical step seemed to be the concert circuit. While I was on the radio, my agent was Charlie Wagner, and later, Dick Dorso. (Unfortunately, Dick's biggest claim to fame today is that his business partner was Marty Melcher, who married Doris Day and flushed all her money down the drain.) When I left radio, I got a call from an agent who was well connected in the concert field, Horace Parmelee of Columbia Artists Management. He wanted to know if he could represent me. We hit it off right away, and I signed with him. When I met him, he was probably already in his late sixties. "Uncle" Horace was a real impresario, and one of the sweetest men who ever lived. He gave his personal attention to so many little details and treated me almost like his daughter; he wouldn't make a move, wouldn't tell a concert presenter even "maybe," until he had discussed the deal with me first. Uncle Horace had dozens of neckties, and whenever I made a lunch date with him, I'd look across the table and try to figure out how many things on his plate would wind up on his tie. He made a mess every single time, and when he'd dab at the tie with his handkerchief, he'd just smear it around until it made a bigger stain. Uncle Horace like to joke around, too. He lived in a big apartment house at Columbus Circle, right above the great Met soprano Zinka Milanov, and he used to open his windows and play my records full blast, just to get under her skin.

Once I'd signed with him, Uncle Horace lost no time in getting me launched on the concert circuit. I had an edge over a lot of other singers because my radio show had made me such a familiar name that it was fairly easy to sell me to concert presenters. Columbia Artists had a famous Community Concerts division that was responsible for much of the musical activity that took place in small and medium-size towns. Many big opera stars spent a lot of time on this circuit. Back then, there weren't that many regional opera companies, and the fees at the Met, even for the biggest names, weren't all that much. So Community Concerts was a good way of making extra money. The circuit also had the advantage of introducing musicians who weren't well known to audiences in out-of-the-way places. Even though they didn't like to admit it, Columbia made a practice of block bookings. If a local concert committee wanted Lawrence Tibbett or Risë Stevens, it would have to agree to present a couple of unknowns from Columbia's roster on the same series. Eventually, Columbia dominated the university market, too, and that lasted until the '60s, when students started demanding rock groups instead of opera. The local ladies' concert groups died out after a while, and by the end of the '60s Community Concerts wasn't such a big deal any more. But it was terrific while it lasted.

Now that I was getting booked for recitals, I had to find a good accompanist. In the late forties, someone recommended a young man from Kansas named George Trovillo, who had been playing for the Canadian contralto Jean Watson for a couple of years. We almost got together in 1949, when I was preparing to go to South America for a recital tour. But George had another offer to be accompanist for the tenor James Melton, and it was too good to turn down. George and I decided that he should go ahead, even though it would delay our working together for another two years. George had some pretty wild stories to tell about his association with Melton, who loved to play to the audience. Every time they did a recital together, Melton would spot some white-haired old lady in one of the front rows of the theater, step down from the stage, and go over and put his arm around her. "You remind me so much of my mother," he'd say, "that I'd like to sing this song for you." And he'd launch into "Mother Machree" or some other old Irish sob-job. Poor George used to die a thousand deaths during those performances.

George also played for Roberta Peters, Cesare Valletti, and Jussi Björling. The word "accompanying" doesn't do justice to George's talent. He was my collaborator, and we worked together well into the 1960s, when he moved to San Diego with

Bill Graham, an actor who'd played the lead in the original New York production of *Little Mary Sunshine*.

In our years together, George and I crisscrossed North America, performing in big cities and tiny places I'd never heard of before—Hattiesburg, Mississippi; Hutchinson, Kansas; Moose Jaw, Saskatchewan; Ames, Iowa; Minot, North Dakota. We played many of these towns in the dead of winter, when the temperature was not to be believed. Once when we were in Winnipeg, I saw something I'd never seen before. It was so cold that the fronts of cars were wrapped in canvas to keep their batteries warm. Another time we were in Tampa, Florida, during a cold snap, and since the auditorium was freezing, I shocked the audience by wearing my mink coat onstage for the whole performance.

To get from one place to the other, a lot of times George and I had to stay up most of the night. We'd finish a concert around eleven o'clock, and the train to the next town might be leaving at two or three in the morning, so we'd head back to the hotel, pack our bags, and go down to the train station to wait. I learned things I'd never known about, and some of them were pretty awful. I'll never forget the shock of going to the Deep South and seeing the water fountains marked "Whites Only." That was a first for me.

Conditions varied widely from one auditorium to another. I sang in all sizes of concert halls. In Eugene, Oregon, George and I were booked into an old wreck of a place where the local university held its basketball games. Naturally, since we were in Oregon, it started to rain. The roof of the place was leaking, and as I sang, I could hear the rain falling on the stage around me. Somebody who worked backstage decided he would do me a big favor and put a pail on the stage to catch the drips, so as I sang "Pace, pace, mio Dio" from *La forza del destino*, the rain plunked into the bucket all the while. Probably the lowest point was an auditorium on one of the Great Lakes. The main attractions there were horse shows, and George and I had to perform on a dirt floor, making our way through Schubert and Poulenc while we breathed in the aroma of horse manure.

Then there was a recital up in Maine, at the Bangor Auditorium, which resembled a big old cow shed. Right in the middle of one of my songs, the lights went out. We finished the piece, and since I felt that we had to acknowledge the darkness, I said to the audience, "Sorry, ladies and gentlemen—we don't know what happened. Until the lights come back on, let's all sing." So we sang "The Last Rose of Summer" and a bunch of other chestnuts, but the lights didn't come back on. Finally, fire trucks pulled up, and the firemen threw open the big side doors of the auditorium and shone the lights inside so the audience could see to make its way out.

While I was singing recitals, I was also getting lots of bookings as soloist with symphony orchestras. I know a lot of great concert singers were actually happier on the opera stage. Just standing and singing bored them to death. That's something I can't understand. First of all, in a concert, the whole setup is stripped down to the basics—no tacky costumes, bad lighting, or rickety sets to worry about. It's just you, the conductor, the orchestra, sometimes a chorus and a few other soloists. Also, concert singers earn one hell of a lot more money than opera singers do.

It might seem tricky to go from radio, where I sang to nothing but a microphone, to singing in front of a concert audience, but I don't remember having trouble making the switch. I concentrated on the words, my breathing, keeping my voice forward and sending it out, as I'd always done. I had a big voice, but I didn't abuse it. Miss Mac had taught me that when the orchestra builds in volume, it has nothing to do with the singer. You keep the same timbre, the same quality, and don't get caught up in the wall of sound building around you. If you do, you won't have anything left by the time you get to the climax. When I felt the orchestra swelling on a big climactic phrase and going past my head out into the audience, I didn't try to compete with it. I thought of myself as another instrument, usually a cello.

The challenge of singing concerts is that you're totally exposed. As a result, the conductor can make you either sound sensational or look like an idiot. I'd have to say that for the most part, I had good luck with conductors. I learned from many of them, and a few became close friends. For the most part, though, I didn't pay much attention to them.

It's best for a singer when the conductor has a crisp, clear beat, but during my early days at CBS, I worked with several who were impossible to follow. Over at NBC, I sang many times on *The Bell Telephone Hour*, conducted by Donald Voorhees. We would rehearse, and things would be fine, more or less. We'd break for dinner, and as Don headed out the door, one of the guys in the orchestra would yell, "Hey, Don! Where are you drinking your dinner tonight?" A couple of hours later, he'd stumble back, and the fun would begin. He'd weave back and forth at the podium, blowing whiskey fumes in my direction, and his beat was all over the place. After a few shows with Don, I made it a point to count every measure carefully, no matter who was waving the baton.

While I was still on the radio, I worked with several major-league conductors. One was Leopold Stokowski. A hypnotic conductor who could get amazing results from his orchestra, "Stoki" was named music director of the Philadelphia Orchestra in 1912. Right away, he fired thirty-two of the players. Before long, he had reshaped the group completely and created the sound that would put the Philadelphia Orchestra on the map.

Stoki heard me singing on the radio and sent word that he wanted me to record Wagner's *Wesendonck* Lieder with him. I didn't know any of the songs, so he taught them to me line by line. Sometimes we would have to go over a single line all afternoon until he was satisfied. I hate to think what those early coaching sessions must have been like. The *Wesendonck* songs were so passionate, and what the hell did I know about such things? Only what I read in dirty books. All told, we worked on the songs for over four months before we went into the recording studio. Some critics attacked Stoki for having inconsistent tempi, but I never had that problem with him when we were preparing the *Wesendonck*. He had a tight grip on the music, and he resisted the temptation to get too carried away. By the time Stoki finally pummeled me into shape and we got a date in the recording studios at Manhattan Center on West Thirty-fourth Street, we ran up against a major problem. The recording engineers announced that they were going on strike. We had booked our studio time for the day before the strike was to go into effect. We needed to have everything wrapped up by midnight, or we'd be out of luck. Playing Beat the Clock wasn't exactly the best way to make my recording debut with Stoki, but somehow I managed to get through the last bars of the final song, "Träume," at just a few minutes before midnight.

During my early years of concertizing, I sang the Immolation Scene with Pierre Monteux and the Montreal Symphony. Monteux had been the music director of the San Francisco Symphony for many years, and he had a huge reputation. You couldn't miss Monteux, with his black hair and white moustache. He was touchy about rumors that his hair was dyed, and he was very proud of his moustache, which he kept beautifully combed. Monteux's wife, Doris Hodgkins, definitely ran the show at home, and a lot of times she tried to call the shots with the San Francisco Symphony, too. Once, she insisted that all the men in the orchestra grow moustaches because Papa, as she called her husband, had one.

I was scared stiff at the thought of working with Monteux, but he couldn't have been nicer. For the concert with the Montreal Symphony, we performed in an auditorium on the second floor of a boys' school. We had to do the concert two nights in a row because there weren't enough seats in the auditorium to accommodate the ticket demand. I still remember his famous beat—very small, clear, and precise. Just because it was Wagner didn't mean he had to use grand gestures.

We were both staying at the Ritz, and after we finished the first concert, Monteux said to me, "I will take you back to the hotel. Will you have something to eat with me?" When we arrived at the Ritz, we headed for the bar, where a waiter came to our table and said, "Will you have the usual, Maestro?" Monteux nodded. I figured the usual was a martini or a Manhattan, but it turned out to be a bowl of corn flakes. For me, that humanized him so. As he sat there spooning up his cereal, I said, "Maestro, it's such a privilege for me to be singing with you. I've admired you for so long." And he said, "My dear, just remember, a Frenchman cannot conduct Wagner." I wanted to say, "Well, gee . . . it sounded OK to me."

It's funny how often it's something like a bowl of corn flakes, and not a musical moment, that I remember about a conductor. Whenever I see a Dixie cup, I think of Arturo Toscanini. I sang with him only once, in March 1952. He had decided, after years of doing Beethoven's Ninth Symphony in concert, to make a recording of it. The Beethoven Ninth was one of Toscanini's favorite pieces, and when he asked me to sing the soprano part, I jumped at the chance. (I always enjoyed singing the Beethoven Ninth, because there wasn't much to my part, and I'd have enough energy left to go out after the concert.)

There was a lot of advance publicity surrounding Toscanini's recording of the symphony. Everyone thought it was going to be one of the great recordings of the century. Two performances were scheduled in Carnegie Hall, and then the recording was to be done in two three-hour sessions. Toscanini was eighty-five at the time. He seemed very vital to me, but at dress rehearsal in Carnegie Hall, he slipped and fell forward off the podium. Several of the orchestra players tried to help him up, but he cursed at them and waved them away, telling them he could get up by himself.

The performances went well, but Toscanini wasn't satisfied, and he was determined to get everything right for the recording. On the day of the first session, we rehearsed again and again before the first take. Toscanini got frustrated and yelled at the musicians, but he wasn't really yelling *at* them. He was trying to give directions in both Italian and English, and he would get upset with himself when he couldn't make himself understood.

I'd never seen a conductor so deeply buried in the music. At the point where the soprano part goes up to high B, the engineers in the control room asked him for a level on my voice. All they needed were three or four bars, but Toscanini was so involved, he just kept going. Nobody had the nerve to stop him. I had already sung the section several times, and here I was blowing my brains out, just so they could get a level—but Toscanini kept going straight through to the end. Then he put down his baton and, all of a sudden, snapped his head around and yelled up at the control room, "WHAT DO YOU MAKE HER WORK SO HARD FOR?"

He kept redoing different sections, especially the beginning of the final movement, right before the choral section. "With one more drop of blood," he said, "perhaps we can come a little nearer to what Beethoven wanted." (We killed ourselves that evening to get the right results; nowadays they think nothing of tracking in different parts separately.) When we finally finished, Toscanini slipped into his white terrycloth robe and invited the soloists up to his dressing room for Champagne. The problem was, he had only one bottle. He poured a couple of swallows each into several Dixie cups and passed them around for all of us.

One year later, when I was expecting my second child, Toscanini's son Walter telephoned me and said, "Papa wants to ask if you would do the *Missa Solemnis.*

"Oh, thank you, Walter," I said, "but I can't. I'm about to have a baby."

"Oh, God," said Walter. "Wait a minute," and he put down the phone. Finally he came back and said, "Papa says you can't." It was probably one of the few times the Maestro didn't get his way. I had my daughter, Kathleen, and Lois Marshall got the *Missa Solemnis.*

Another fine singer's conductor was Maurice Abravanel. One concert I'll always remember was the Immolation Scene from *Götterdämmerung,* which I performed in Salt Lake City with Abravanel and the Utah Symphony. I had known Maurice in New York, where he successfully conducted ballet and Broadway musicals. For this particular performance of the Immolation Scene, we were at the Mormon Tabernacle. The acoustics were quite bad, since the Tabernacle is so big and the rear of it is open, and the players were having trouble hearing each other. By the time we started rehearsing the Immolation Scene it was evening, and there wasn't a soul left in the place. The orchestra kept building to the climax of the scene, and the sound kept rolling out into that great, empty space. I reached the end of Brünnhilde's part, and the orchestra continued to play to the final bars. I looked over at Abravanel. Tears were rolling down his face as he led the final pages of the scene. There wasn't anything but the night and the music.

Alfredo Antonini wasn't really much of a conductor, but he *was* colorful. He was a staff conductor at CBS when I had my radio show, and several years later, in the early 1950s, I worked with him again at Lewisohn Stadium, in Manhattan. Also on the program were Richard Tucker and Beverly Sills, who would become a close friend of mine. One of the arias I had been scheduled to sing was "Casta diva," from Bellini's *Norma*. Norma is one of the most challenging roles in the soprano repertory, and "Casta diva" is a killer, since you have to open the opera with it. I never sang *Norma* onstage, although Carol Fox was always trying to get me to do it for her when she was general director of Lyric Opera of Chicago. Anyway, there I was, rehearsing "Casta diva," cabaletta and all, struggling to keep up with Antonini's breakneck pace. Finally he stopped and said, "Now, Farrell, when we do this in performance, I no wait-a for you! *I no wait-a for you!*"

Someday, I thought, a conductor will call me "*Miss* Farrell," and then I'll know I've really made it. We did the performance, and guess what? Antonini no wait-a for me. I barely had enough breath to get to the end of the aria, and that cured me of any temptation to say yes to Carol Fox's offer.

I sang under Dmitri Mitropoulos several times during his tenure as music director of the New York Philharmonic (1949–58). Our first group of concerts is the one I remember best. Mitropoulos was eager to have the Philharmonic reach beyond the regular subscription audiences at Carnegie Hall. So in September 1950, thanks to his persistence, the orchestra was booked into the Roxy Theater, a huge old movie palace on Seventh Avenue between Fiftieth and Fifty-first Streets. In between showings of a Tyrone Power picture called *The Black Rose*, I sang "Un bel dì" and "The Last Rose of Summer." Originally, we were booked for only a week, but audiences poured in, and we added another week. The second week, I sang "Pace, pace." The arias were a snap; the real test was "The Last Rose of Summer." The entire orchestra just sat on its hands while I sang, accompanied only by a harpist. It apparently created quite a powerful effect in the Roxy, but it played hell with my nerves. "The Last

Rose of Summer" is tough under any conditions, and here we were in the Roxy, with the harpist on Fiftieth Street and me on Fifty-first Street. By the end of the two weeks, I had racked up fifty-six performances with the Philharmonic, which helped me set a record, eventually, as the singer who had appeared most often with the orchestra. (I have no idea if the record still holds, although I think those fifty-six performances probably gave me a head start on just about anybody.)

The first show at the Roxy started at eleven o'clock in the morning, and I had to change my gown before each of the four daily shows. I pretty much lived at the theater for those two weeks, but in between shows I caught up on my reading, and the time passed quickly. One evening several sober-looking men wearing business suits knocked on my dressing-room door and announced themselves as Secret Service agents. I couldn't figure out what they wanted until they informed me that President Truman's daughter, Margaret, was in the audience and wanted to come back and say hello. This was around the time that Miss Truman was trying to carve out her not-too-successful singing career. She came rushing backstage and fell all over me, telling me how she idolized me and hoped one day she would have a career like mine. The Secret Service men stood by the entire time, watching every move I made. What did they think I was going to do—give her a lesson?

Some people assume that a conductor has to be a tyrant in order to maintain discipline in the orchestra, but most of the maestros I sang under were supportive and sympathetic. They understood that the clarinet section isn't necessarily going to play in tune if you just stand there and keep yelling at them. Dmitri Mitropoulos was one of the kindest conductors I ever sang under. He was a very religious man who always wore a cross, and his home was filled with statues and paintings of St. Francis of Assisi. When we played the two-week engagement at the Roxy, he donated his entire salary to one of the big Catholic charitable organizations. Shortly after the Roxy gig, I was reunited with Mitropoulos and the Philharmonic for performances of Darius Milhaud's *Les choéphores*. This was again part of Mitropoulos's campaign to expand the orchestra's horizons: He wanted to program more dramatic works, which weren't all that common at the time. This turned out to be a very successful move for the Philharmonic, and Mitropoulos was soon piling cantatas and operas onto the season's schedule. No question that the most challenging one—for both the audience and the performers—had to be *Wozzeck*, which had its U.S. premiere in Philadelphia in 1931, and entered the Philharmonic's repertory in April 1951.

These days, *Wozzeck* turns up at the Met fairly regularly, but in the early 1950s, you didn't come across a performance of it very often. I had sung excerpts from it on Bernard Herrmann's *Invitation to Music*, but this time I would be performing the entire opera. I worked on it with Miss Mac and with Hermann Weigert, a wonderful coach who was married to Astrid Varnay. Memorizing an entire twelve-tone score was murder, and I had to concentrate like blazes to drum the unfamiliar pitches into my ear. Mack Harrell, who was Wozzeck, or Frederick Jagel, who did a terrific job as the Drum Major, would come to the end of a phrase, and I would stand there sweating it, thinking, "OK, now my line is next, and it's three and a half tones above Mack's last note, and that would be a D . . ." Still, by the time the first day of rehearsal rolled around, I thought I had my part pretty much under my belt.

I wasn't prepared for how well Mitropoulos knew *Wozzeck*. At that first rehearsal, he showed up without a score; he had committed every note to memory. The guys in the orchestra just sat there with their mouths hanging open as Mitropoulos said, "Okay, now subdivide the first three bars . . ." We finished the rehearsal, and a group of us got in a cab to go to lunch. Mitropoulos turned to me and said, "So, what's the matter with you?"

"What do you mean, what's the matter with me?" I asked. "This music is hard."

"It's *not* hard," he snapped. "I counted on you, out of everyone here, to know your part perfectly."

"Well," I said, "gee . . . I *almost* do."

For Mitropoulos, "almost" wasn't good enough. He told me about his early years in Greece, when his family was too poor to buy scores. Instead, he had to go to the library and check them out. He pored over them for hours, and since he wasn't sure he'd ever be able to afford to buy them, he made sure he memorized them.

We did three performances at Carnegie Hall, and both the press and public were wild over them. People still talk about that *Wozzeck* as one of the most exciting concerts of the time, and fortunately, Columbia preserved it on a recording.

Some conductors, of course, have no stick technique at all. I loved Arthur Fiedler dearly, but he was one of the world's worst conductors. I purposely avoided looking at him when I was singing with the Boston Pops—because if I had looked, I would have been lost around the first bend. If you watch some of the old Boston Pops telecasts closely, you'll see that lots of the orchestra musicians didn't watch him, either. They'd been playing together so long they listened carefully and followed each other.

Arthur could be abusive to the players, and even more so to his poor wife, but he was always very sweet to me. The first time I sang with him was at Massey Hall, in Toronto. I was thrilled to be working with him, but through the excitement I did notice one thing I'd never seen a conductor do before. When Fiedler came out onstage, he didn't leave. There was a reason for that: If he had walked offstage, he'd probably never have been able to find his way back. For example, when we finished the performance in Toronto and exited into the wings, I saw his valet standing by with a towel over his arm and a bottle on a tray.

"Don't come near me!" Fiedler said, waving me away. "I have a terrible cold." I believed him, but after I sang with him a few more times, I figured out that the bottle was filled with whiskey.

Years later, I did a Boston Pops telecast with him. In the green room at Symphony Hall, he had a desk where he kept his bottle in a locked drawer. You'd sit down to have a chat with him, and he'd unlock the drawer, pour himself a glass of whiskey, and give it a stir with his baton. Then he'd lick the baton, smack his lips, and carry on with what he was saying.

Over the years, I worked with a lot of talented young musicians, and it was wonderful to watch them go on to big careers. Then there were the ones who later surprised me by how far they got. Once, in the early 1970s, when I was teaching at Indiana University, I was booked to perform an evening of George Gershwin's music with the Buffalo Philharmonic, to be conducted by the orchestra's young music director, Michael Tilson Thomas. I had never worked with him before, but his career was rising quickly, and I had heard nothing but good things about him. Michael flew out to Bloomington so we could run through the program at my house. I had already told him which key I would use for each song, and I assumed everything was all set to go.

I knew I was in trouble as soon as Michael arrived at our house and sat down at the piano. He launched into the first song, "I'll Build a Stairway to Paradise," and it was deadly—no pulse, no life—Michael played it as if he'd never heard it before.

"Michael," I said, "Uh . . . it's so square. I can't sing it that way."

"Well, that's the way it's written," he said.

"But I don't sing it that way. Besides, it's not the right key for me."

"Well, that's the key it's written in," he insisted, "and anyway, I can't play it in the key you want."

"I have an idea, Michael. Let's have dinner."

So we had dinner, and Michael monopolized the conversation all evening long. He told Bob and me all about his grandfather, who had performed in drag in the Yiddish theater. Bob sat across the table glaring at him and getting quieter by the minute. I wanted to laugh, but I didn't dare. We finished dinner, and Michael and I said good night.

The next day, Bob called my agent in New York, Herbert Barrett, to try to get me out of the engagement. When Herbert pointed out that we had a signed contract, I got an idea. I called Joey Singer, a talented kid who played for the jazz class I taught at Indiana, and asked if he would like to accompany me. We went to Buffalo, and Michael led the orchestra for the first half of the program. Then they all left the stage, and Joey and I took over the second half. I don't think Michael said a word to me, especially after Joey and I brought down the house. The next morning, the local music critic wrote a review that asked the question: "What in the world was Eileen Farrell doing there all by herself, killing us with all her songs?" I can imagine how Michael must have loved that. That remains the one and only time that we almost worked together.

I don't like to fight with anyone—not my friends, my family, not even conductors—so I was delighted that the whole M.T.T. affair could be resolved so smoothly. It didn't always turn out that way. Once, I was singing the Verdi Requiem at a spring music festival in Ann Arbor. Patrice Munsel was scheduled to close the festival, but she came down with a cold, and they asked me if I would perform the final concert. The conductor of the festival was Eugene Ormandy, the legendary music director of the Philadelphia Orchestra. We settled on a group of arias, and Ormandy told me there was just enough time to send to Detroit for the scores. By the time they arrived, we were barely able to squeeze in a half-hour rehearsal with the orchestra. Still, the concert went off without a hitch.

After the performance, Mr. Sink, the man who ran the Ann Arbor festival, had a party at his house. You know the kind—a green-cream-cheese-sandwich-and-pissy-pink-punch party. Ormandy was a tiny man, and maybe his size was the reason he couldn't hold his liquor. By the time I arrived at the party, he was already plowed. The atmosphere got more and more tense as Ormandy came out with one off-color joke after another. With every joke, people laughed less and less. Poor Mr. and Mrs. Sink looked miserable. Finally, in desperation, Ormandy turned to me and said, "Tell me, Farrell, how much do you weigh?"

"I'm not going to tell you, Maestro," I said. "After all, I wouldn't think of asking you in front of all these people how tall you are."

At least with Ormandy, it was the booze talking. George Szell couldn't even use that as an excuse. I was scheduled to perform the Verdi Requiem with Szell and the Cleveland Orchestra. It was quite a group of soloists: Nell Rankin, Richard Tucker, George London, and me. It should have been a great experience, but when we got to the dress rehearsal, Szell stopped cold in the middle of the "Libera me."

"STOP! STOP! YOU'RE TOO LOUD! GOD! SING SOFTER! THIS IS A REQUIEM, FOR GOD'S SAKE!"

It was the only time that a conductor actually screamed at me in rehearsal. Szell was a bully to the core, and he yelled at the orchestra players all the time, so I guess they were used to it. I wasn't.

"If you wanted a softer singer," I said, "why didn't you hire one?"

Szell gave me a drop-dead look. For the rest of the rehearsal, he didn't say one word to me. I left Severance Hall that day in a rage. I was supposed to have lunch with my good friend Beverly Sills, who was at the time living in Shaker Heights with her husband, publishing heir Peter Greenough, and his children from a previous marriage. Beverly later told me that all morning she had been preparing the kids for meeting me. She told them that a great lady was coming for lunch, and they had to be dressed up and on their best behavior. They were all waiting for me out in front of the house when my taxi pulled up. I'd had the entire ride to build up a good head of steam, and the minute my feet hit the pavement, I exploded.

"Shit!" I yelled as I slammed my taxi door so hard I nearly took it off its hinges. "That goddamned Szell! Where in the hell's the whiskey?"

Just then I realized that the kids were standing there. Their eyes were the size of fifty-cent pieces, and Beverly was smiling nervously. She took me by the arm and ushered me into the house before I did any more damage, sent the children out of the room, poured me a stiff drink, and listened patiently while I continued to rant about Szell.

Szell had the last word. After the performance, he passed me in the hallway. Without breaking stride, he muttered, "It went well—despite everything."

Bitch.

I sang with James Levine only once, in an all-Wagner concert at Chicago's Ravinia Festival, where he was music director. Granted, he was quite young at the time, and I suppose I'd been spoiled by having Lenny Bernstein conduct me in so many Wagner performances—it doesn't get any better than that. I don't recall that Levine made any mistakes, but something about his music making just left me cold. He wasn't exactly my type of personality, either. There didn't seem to be any joy in the process. He reminded me a little bit of a Juilliard know-it-all who had never really grown up. At the first rehearsal, he came up to me and said, "You know, I remember when you sang *Gioconda* on the Met tour when I was just a kid. I sat up in the top balcony and followed every note you sang with a score." I thought, Oh, yeah, I can just *picture* you, a little know-it-all teenager holed up in the balcony. Levine stopped short of telling me whether he *liked* my Gioconda, but I'm sure that if I had held one dotted quarter a second too long, he would have been on the case.

I worked with Erich Leinsdorf many times in concert, and in 1960 he conducted my Met debut in *Alceste*. We got on very well, and at some point he got it into his head that he wanted me to make a recording of *Madama Butterfly*.

"I can't," I said. "It's such beautiful music, I couldn't ever get through it without crying."

"That's no reason," he said. "I don't believe you. Come sing it for me."

So we got together, and partway through "Un bel dì," I choked up. "See?" I said. "I'd never be able to do a complete recording. It's such a sad story, and the music is so gorgeous. It'd just be too much for me."

"OK, OK, I believe you," he said, "but I still don't think it's a good reason for not doing the record."

There usually wasn't time for me to get to know most of the conductors I worked with very well, but there were two who were especially close to my heart—Thomas Schippers and Leonard Bernstein. They had some things in common. They were both American—Tommy was from Kalamazoo, Michigan, and Lenny was from Lawrence, Massachusetts—and they were among the few American-born conductors to become music directors of major symphony orchestras at the time. They were both terrifically ambitious men, musically and socially. And most important, as far as I was concerned, they were the two best singers' conductors I ever worked with. They both had a great understanding of how the human voice functioned, and I did some of the best singing of my career with them.

I met Tommy first. Before my 1949 recital tour of South America, I had to scramble to find an accompanist. Someone recommended a young pianist named Thomas Schippers. I'd never heard of him, but we met, and he played for me. I told him right on the spot that I'd take him to South America with me.

Tommy was only nineteen, but he was already an incredibly sophisticated musician. He lived for music, and his devotion had caused him a lot of suffering; his parents didn't quite know how to deal with such an artistically gifted boy. But even though Tommy was a polished musician, he didn't know much about anything else. In fact, it didn't take me long to figure out that he'd never been five feet from horseshit in his life. When we left on our tour, we flew out of Newark International Airport. The flight was called, and no Tommy. Bob scoured the airport looking for him, and finally, just as the gate was about to close, Tommy strolled up, casually eating an ice cream cone. He didn't have the slightest idea what time the flight was leaving. This was how things went for the rest of the trip.

In Maracaibo, Tommy and I stayed in an old hotel with no screens on the windows, which meant that about 1,465 bugs were constantly swarming in and out of the rooms. Outside, you could hear the donkeys' hooves and the squeals of children who played naked in the streets. I was too upset to soak up much local color. I had left my little Robbie behind on Staten Island, and

I spent most of the time crying, positive I was never going to see him again. Fortunately, I had Tommy with me, and if anyone ever needed mothering, he did. One evening I went down to his room to pick him up for dinner and found him standing in his bathroom running an electric razor over his face. There was a big drain in the middle of the floor where all the water from the shower went, and Tommy was shaving away, never noticing that he was standing in a huge puddle of water in his bare feet. I let out a scream, and from that moment, I never let him out of my sight. I was afraid he might wander off and never come back. Mostly all we did was sit in the room and play cards and drink the cheap South American beer, which was awful.

Tommy was terribly naïve in some ways, shrewd in others. While we were in South America, he used every spare minute to study the score of Gian Carlo Menotti's opera *The Consul*. He planned to audition for Gian Carlo as soon as we returned to New York. I had known Gian Carlo for some time and liked him very much. I believe we met for the first time when I sang Samuel Barber's *Knoxville: Summer of 1915* on Benny Herrmann's *Invitation to Music*. (I adored Sam, who was such an elegant gentleman, always beautifully turned out. Later on, he accompanied me when I performed his cycle of French songs, *Mélodies passagères,* at Dumbarton Oaks, in Washington, D.C.) Sam and Gian Carlo had been together for many years, and the three of us saw a lot of each other. Gian Carlo had a big group of buddies who used to do a lot of networking before it was called "networking," and they seemed to me a little bit exclusive—as if they were members of a private club.

I thought Tommy was so gifted, and one night while we were playing cards and drinking cheap beer, "Mother Reagan" decided to give him a little unsolicited advice. "You know, Tommy," I said, "you have so much talent. You're young, you're

That's Tommy Schippers right
behind Lenny Bernstein's left
shoulder; Tommy was just a kid, and
this photo really shows how eager he
was to have a career like Lenny's.
Photography by Howard S. Babbitt,
Jr., courtesy of *Opera News*.

good looking. You don't need to get in with Gian Carlo and all his friends. Don't do that just to get ahead in the music business. Do it on your own." He listened carefully to every word I said, and oh, he appreciated it so much.

Well—*guess what happened?*

Tommy did get to conduct *The Consul* on Broadway, and it did turn out to be an important career boost for him. In 1951, he conducted the original telecast of Gian Carlo's *Amahl and the Night Visitors* on NBC. His relationship with Gian Carlo lasted for many years, and all the while, Gian Carlo continued to live with Sam at Capricorn, their house in Mt. Kisco, New York. Sam and Gian Carlo remained close; they were both sophisticated men of the world, relaxed and at ease with each other, and more on the same wavelength than Tommy and Gian Carlo were. Tommy was more of a boy-wonder type, outgoing and high-energy, sort of nipping at Gian Carlo's heels and pushing him along. Pretty soon, Tommy's conducting career went into high gear. He had a special gift for opera. It's amazing to think that only six years after our South American tour, he made his debuts at both La Scala and the Met. He also had a hand in the founding of Gian Carlo's Festival of Two Worlds in Spoleto, Italy.

In 1957 I did a recording with Tommy and the London Philharmonia Orchestra, *Eileen Farrell Sings Grand Opera*. I think that recording contains some of my very best singing, but it's a wonder we ever got it off the ground, because Tommy had terrible problems with the London Philharmonia. To be honest, the orchestra hated his guts. The players, particularly the cello section, would ignore all his dynamic instructions. He'd stop to explain once more what he wanted them to do, and the minute they started to play, they'd ignore him all over again. The morning after one especially difficult session, Tommy called me at my hotel and asked if he could have breakfast with me. When we met, he said, "Eileen, I want you to tell me honestly. Why does the orchestra dislike me so?"

I knew the reason. Whenever Tommy addressed the orchestra, he started to speak in hemi-demi-semi-quavers. He put on an affected English accent and tried to talk down to them, to show them who was in charge. He was just a scared little kid from Kalamazoo trying to cover up his insecurity, and the people in the orchestra were smart enough to figure him out. I decided it would be in his best interest to level with him.

"Tommy," I said, "there's one reason only that the orchestra doesn't like you. It's because you're such a little shit."

He looked at me as if I'd slapped him right across the face, but I went on.

"It's not necessary for you to put on airs, honey," I said. "Why do you think you're on the conductor's podium and they're sitting there? You're loaded with talent. Use it. It's yours. Just do us all a favor and be yourself."

We managed to get through the rest of the recording, which included "Divinités du Styx" from *Alceste* and "To This We've Come" from Gian Carlo's *The Consul*, which I often sang at the close of my recital programs. In the opera, Magda, a young wife and mother, is trying desperately to secure visas for herself and her family so they can get out of the police state where they're trapped. In "To This We've Come," Magda finally breaks down under the constant delays and red tape and lashes out at the consul's unfeeling secretary. Gian Carlo wrote some beautiful words for the end of the aria:

> Oh! The day will come, I know,
> when our hearts aflame will burn your paper chains.
> Warn the Consul, Secretary, warn him.
> That day neither ink nor seal shall cage our souls.
> That day will come!

It was always difficult for me to reach that climax and make it as fiery as it needed to be without breaking down and crying. Just hearing a certain chord can reduce me to tears, and Gian Carlo had written a beautiful, sweeping opening to the last section of "To This We've Come" that was always a struggle for me to get past. Recording it with Tommy was nerve-wracking because Gian Carlo was sitting right there, watching and listening the whole time. Fortunately, it turned out well, and I'm happy that "To This We've Come" is an aria that audiences still associate with me.

Several years after we recorded *Eileen Farrell Sings Grand Opera*, Tommy was scheduled to do another recording in London. By this time he had a big international conducting career. One morning I got a phone call from him.

"I'm on my way to London, Eileen," he said. "Tell me again—what did I do the last time that I shouldn't have?" He'd had our conversation on his mind for all those years, and even though he was famous now and didn't need to ask anyone for advice, he was open to suggestions. That's a sign of a pretty big man.

Tommy's career was thriving, but in time, most conductors want a permanent post with an orchestra or opera house, and he was no exception. Tommy was gifted, movie-star handsome, and had tremendous presence, and I thought he was a natural to become principal conductor of the New York Philharmonic when Lenny Bernstein left. Of course, in those days it helped if you were married and people thought of you as a solid, straight-arrow citizen. This may not have been fair, but it was in keeping with the times. Tommy probably had all of this figured out, and deep down, he knew that in order to get a permanent conducting spot, it would only help him if he got married.

Nonie (Elaine) Phipps was a beautiful, charming young woman from one of New York's most distinguished families. She was a descendant of W. R. Grace, New York's first Irish Catholic

Tommy Schippers after he made it.
He always wore those velour shirts
when he rehearsed. Courtesy of
Opera News.

mayor. Tommy had known Nonie and her family for quite some time, and eventually they became an item. Her family donated a lot of money to various arts organizations, which gave Tommy another leg up in pursuing the job at Philharmonic. I don't believe for one second that this was totally an ambitious move on Tommy's part, the way some people said it was—I honestly think that he loved Nonie deeply, and she loved him. In 1965 they were married, and in 1970 he was named music director of the Cincinnati Symphony Orchestra. It may not have been the Philharmonic, but it was an extremely prestigious position. (Tommy was the ninth music director in the orchestra's history.) He and Nonie moved into a big old Victorian house that the symphony bought for them, and they fixed it up beautifully. The backyard ran into the Hyde Park Country Club, and Tommy played golf every day, becoming part of Cincinnati society. He seemed to have everything he wanted.

In the early 1970s, Jess Thomas and I were engaged to sing a Wagner concert with the Cincinnati Symphony, with Tommy conducting. After the concert, we had dinner with Tommy and Nonie at their house. I can still picture how spectacular they looked together. What Jess and I didn't know was that Nonie had terminal cancer. She died not long after that, and Tommy was inconsolable. A bit later, I did another concert with him, and I noticed that he looked thin and haggard. Soon I heard that he, too, had been diagnosed with cancer, and on December 16, 1977, my beautiful, talented friend was dead at forty-seven.

Today, Tommy isn't remembered as well as he deserves to be, probably because he lived in the shadow of Leonard Bernstein. Hands down, Lenny was the greatest conductor I have ever worked with. After he became music director of the New York Philharmonic in 1958, I was engaged for a number of concerts with the orchestra. By the time we had finished the first set of performances, I could already tell what an impact he'd had on the orchestra. The sections blended so much better than they had under Mitropoulos. The strings had come an especially long way; at times, they sounded like a single instrument. I knew lots of the players—some of them had been in the CBS Symphony—and one day I complimented Lenny on the progress he'd made with them.

"Well, there's a lot I'd like to do here," he said, "but some of these men have been here so long that I wouldn't have the heart to get rid of them." In my experience, that's the way he always worked with musicians. I don't think I ever heard him lose his temper with a single performer. If someone was singing flat, Lenny would say, "Now, that's fine, darling—just think that it's a little higher than it is." He corrected people often, but always in a kind and constructive way.

Lenny, of course, was one of the great Mahler conductors of the century. I don't think I ever sang a note of Mahler in my life, and to this day, I don't have the faintest idea why, because I'm sure I would have loved doing it. But Lenny never asked me to sing Mahler. Mostly, he wanted me for Wagner and Beethoven, and I was thrilled to do it. We did Wagner excerpts in concert performances—I never performed a complete Wagner role on either the concert or opera stage. Years ago, someone quoted me as saying that singing Wagner was like walking through mud in snowshoes, and that remark got around the music business. If I ever did say that, I was probably just being a smart-ass. The truth is, I loved singing Wagner, especially when Lenny was waving the stick.

Twenty years after I had done the *Wesendonck* Lieder with Stokowski, I recorded them again with Lenny. Now I had a much better idea of what the songs were all about. So many conductors just plow through the music and never take the time to break down individual phrases with the singer. Lenny was the ultimate singer's conductor. He breathed right along with me, and he was always bringing out special nuances in Wagner's music that I never would have discovered on my own. He took his time with the *Wesendonck* songs, sculpting one luscious phrase after another. His treatment of Wagner was the most sensuous I have ever heard in my life.

We also did excerpts from *Tristan und Isolde* and *Götterdämmerung*. Here, too, working with Lenny was like taking a seminar in Wagner performance. "Listen, right here," he'd say as the orchestra rehearsed the Prelude to *Tristan*. "That's the first time in the opera that you hear this particular theme. Now think about how it should sound." I had sung Wagner with a lot of conductors by this time—Charles Munch, Maurice Abravanel, Pierre Monteux—but Lenny was opening up a whole new world to me, and it showed in the final results. We recorded the *Wesendonck* songs, along with the Immolation Scene, and won the Grammy Award for Best Classical Recording of 1962.

There are a few pirate tapes floating around of the *Tristan und Isolde* excerpts that Lenny and I performed at Philharmonic Hall over the years. One from 1969, with Jess Thomas as Tristan, is especially wild. I would have loved to do a complete *Tristan* with Lenny. My approach to Isolde was always very lyric—she is, after all, a young Irish princess, and the part should be sung that way. So many sopranos have used a heavy, laser-beam approach to the part, which can be thrilling, all right, but it's not the way I would have done it.

On September 23, 1962, Lenny and the Philharmonic gave a concert for the official opening of Lincoln Center. Philharmonic Hall (now Avery Fisher Hall) was the first of the buildings completed. Lenny put together a special program that included Beethoven's *Missa Solemnis*, the first movement of Mahler's Symphony no. 8, the world premiere of Copland's *Connotations for Orchestra*, and Vaughan Williams's *Serenade to Music*. I sang in the

Beethoven and Vaughan Williams, which had an amazing group of soloists, including Adele Addison, Jennie Tourel, Shirley Verrett-Carter, Lucine Amara, Lili Chookasian, Richard Tucker, Jon Vickers, George London, and Giorgio Tozzi. It was a gala occasion, telecast live, with all kinds of dignitaries in attendance. President Kennedy wasn't one of them, and because it was such an important event, he got plenty of criticism for not showing up. The First Lady was there, though, and the press blasted Lenny for kissing her on the cheek at intermission.

While we were preparing for the concert, Lenny was under a lot of pressure. He wanted this to be a perfect performance, and the person whose reaction worried him most was Harold Schonberg, first critic of *The New York Times*. Lenny was consumed by his fear of this man. We went over and over the music, perfecting each detail, and finally Lenny said, "There! Let Schonberg find fault with *that!*"

Every now and then, Lenny showed that kind of insecurity. He'd had all this success as a conductor and a composer of musicals, ballets, and orchestral music, and with his work in TV, but occasionally he still showed that he had low self-esteem. In the fall of 1961, I went on tour with Lenny and the Philharmonic. After we were finished with a concert, Lenny liked to gather everyone around him in his hotel room. He'd sit in his chair, and the rest of us would sit on the floor, with me right next to him, and he would hold court in a friendly way. I think he felt musicians were extended family.

I had known for some time that Lenny had been involved with men, both before and during his marriage to Felicia Montealegre. In New York, he kept that part of his life completely separate; all he concentrated on was getting the job done. But when we were on tour, I saw him let down his guard a little around one man or another. Lots of people felt sorry for Felicia, but I didn't see her as a victim at all. She got a lot out of that marriage, and being Mrs. Leonard Bernstein was very important to her.

In 1970, Lenny received a lot of negative publicity by hosting a party to raise money for the militant group the Black Panthers. Several members of the group had been arrested for plotting to blow up buildings and assassinate policemen. None of them had a dime, and Lenny was one of the celebrities who took up their cause, helping raise money for their legal defense. I don't know how sincere Lenny was about helping them, or if it was mostly just a pose. I did know that politically he was 180 degrees away from me. I've been a staunch Republican all my life, as was my husband. I was shocked that Lenny was supporting a group that plotted to destroy buildings and people, but he and I never argued politics. He had bigger opponents than me, anyway. Lots of prominent Jewish groups were outraged by his involvement with the Black Panthers because part of their message was downright anti-Semitic. Many people felt the Panthers were taking Lenny for a ride, using him for his fame and money, all the while planning to harm his own people.

One evening in 1970, I arrived at Philharmonic Hall to perform a Wagner concert with Lenny. Various Jewish groups were picketing outside. I got in the elevator and found a policeman stationed there. Police were also positioned backstage and near the dressing rooms. It was pretty frightening being onstage that night, not knowing if someone was going to take a shot at him right in the middle of the Liebestod. I don't know if the audience sensed how scared we were, but they rewarded us with a huge ovation at the end.

Although Tommy Schippers never was a serious threat to him, Lenny probably had reason to be jealous of Tommy from time to time. Tommy was big in the opera world in a way Lenny never was, and I'm sure it rankled when Tommy was chosen to conduct Sam Barber's *Antony and Cleopatra* for the opening of the new Metropolitan Opera House at Lincoln Center in 1966. By then, Lenny was acknowledged as the leading American conductor of that time. Ordinarily, though, Tommy wasn't any competition for Lenny. When Tommy walked into a room, lots of people looked at him because he was so damned good-looking. (I think he made people nervous because he *was* so handsome.) It was different when Lenny walked into a room—he dominated it completely. He was electric; you half-expected to hear "The Star Spangled Banner" struck up in the background.

Later on in the 1970s, I was once again singing with Lenny. By this time, all his years of smoking and drinking had caught up with him, and he was showing his age badly. As we reached a quiet moment in the piece, I happened to look over at him. His face was haggard and gray, and he looked like a man who had been completely used up. I thought, "That's exactly how he's going to look in his coffin." A chill ran right up my spine, and for a few seconds, I completely forgot where I was.

Felicia died of lung cancer in 1978, and I didn't see much of Lenny after that, but he did call me not long after my husband died in 1986. When you got on the telephone with Lenny, it was all over—you could forget about doing anything else for the rest of the day. We talked and talked for over an hour, reliving old times. Then he asked me if I would agree to sing, with him accompanying me at the piano, for an AIDS benefit at Carnegie Hall.

"Lenny, I can't. Bob just died, and I can't even think about singing. It's too hard."

As always, Lenny could talk me into anything. After a few minutes of his coaxing, I agreed to do the concert. I went to his apartment at the Dakota, on West Seventy-second Street, to rehearse the song we had chosen—Lenny's own "Some Other Time" from *On the Town*. I hadn't seen him for several years, and I was shocked to see how awful he looked. His face was lined and more weary-looking than ever, and he wore his shirt open so that it showed most of his chest and the strings of gold chains clanging around his neck. The minute I walked into the apartment, he threw his arms around me and started sobbing on my shoulder.

"I can't believe Bob's dead. I wish I'd known him better," he whimpered. "And I can't believe Felicia's dead. I don't think I can go on without her."

I didn't know exactly what to make of all this. I didn't know exactly what kind of marriage Lenny and Felicia had had. Yet here he was, crying his heart out. Maybe he was afraid to be left alone, or maybe he sensed that time was running out.

It didn't really matter. I sat there holding him while he kept crying. I knew that day that he couldn't possibly live much longer, and on October 14, 1990, he died. I still miss him. His life may have been overly complicated, some of it of his own making, but there was no denying his genius. Of all the conductors I ever worked with, Lenny remains the love of my life.

CHAPTER SEVEN

OB AND I always planned to have more than one child, and in the early 1950s, I got pregnant again. One night, when I was about three months along, I was singing a recital in Baltimore. I was in the middle of a song when suddenly I realized something was wrong. I finished the song and stumbled offstage, but I feared the worst. I had miscarried. The next morning I took the train from Baltimore to Elizabeth, New Jersey, just across the bridge from Staten Island. Bob was there to meet me, and he knew as soon as he saw me that I had bad news.

It wasn't until six years after Robbie was born that our daughter, Kathleen, came along on February 20, 1953. We made the trip to the hospital early in the morning, just as we had with Robbie, and again there was a beautiful sunrise. It was an easy birth, and three weeks later, I sang a recital. When I was pregnant with Robbie, I had gained only nine pounds, mostly because I'd been sick before and after my ovarian surgery. With Kathleen, I gained forty, and it was a long time before I got rid of them.

Kathleen was off to a bumpy start. The day after we brought her home from the hospital, Robbie came down with chicken pox. The doctor assured us that babies are immune to chicken pox, but Kathleen got them too, followed by shingles a month later.

Not that it slowed her down. Robbie was a serious, quiet child, but Kathleen moved like a runaway train. She was unstoppable—she learned to walk and talk early, and she hasn't shut up since. Kathleen was always precocious. Once, when she was a very tiny girl, I took her shopping on Staten Island. A lady walking down the street stopped and knelt down to speak to Kathleen.

"Aren't you the cutest thing?" the woman squealed. "What's your name, darling?"

Kathleen opened her mouth and shouted, "MY NAME IS LILY PONS!" I'd been doing a *Bell Telephone Hour* with Lily, and I guess I'd mentioned her name several times—I knew then, if I hadn't known before, that my little girl listened to every word that came out of my mouth.

Unlike their mother, Robbie and Kathleen were excellent students. Robbie was a perfectionist from the time he started school. He would sit at his desk in his room, working for hours on his homework assignments until everything was *exactly* right. Both of them were avid readers from an early age. Kathleen was at the head of her class all the way through school. In kindergarten, she was upset because school lasted only half a day.

When Kathleen was three, we bought an enormous three-story stucco house at 72 Louis Street on Staten Island. The view from just about anywhere in the house was great. The front looked out on New York harbor, and the kitchen window faced the Statue of Liberty and Manhattan. From the sunroom you could see Sandy Hook, and the back of the third floor gave you a look at Newark Airport. I had a wonderful music room to work

After Kathleen's arrival, 1953.
Personal collection of Eileen Farrell.

in, and there was a huge basement for Bob and a big third-floor playroom for the kids.

I tried never to be away from home for more than two weeks at a time. Looking back, I should have tried to do even better than that. Children need their parents all the time, and I know there were days when both Robbie and Kathleen felt deprived because I wasn't there for a school program or some other big event. (Kathleen was especially hurt that I had to be away for her confirmation.) I think Kathleen had a particular need to have me close by. Once, when I was singing *Trovatore* on Staten Island, she came to the performance. At the breakfast table the morning after, she was very sullen.

"What's the matter with you?" I asked her.

"I had a bouquet of violets for you last night," she said, "but they wouldn't let me come up to the stage and throw them to you."

"I have an idea, honey," I said. I went up to the first landing on our stairway, and Kathleen tossed me the bouquet.

At school, Robbie and Kathleen took a little heat from the other kids because they had a singer for a mom. Once Kathleen invited a friend home for dinner. The next day, she came home madder than a hornet.

"I don't want any more candles on the table at dinnertime," she said.

"Oh, really?" I asked. "Why?"

"Because Mary Jane made fun of us because we have candles on the table, and all the other kids laughed." I had to promise her then and there that whenever her classmates came over, the candles would come off the table.

Fortunately, neither Robbie nor Kathleen wanted to be in the limelight, and occasionally, when they wound up there, they regretted it. In 1960, CBS's *Person to Person* did a segment on me, with a live hookup from our house. We were all a little nervous

Waiting on the Irish princess.
A comb-out for Kathleen, at 72
Louis Street, Staten Island. Personal
collection of Eileen Farrell.

about appearing on coast-to-coast TV, and Robbie made a slip of the tongue that haunted him for years. Charles Collingwood noticed Robbie's husky build and asked him if he played football. Robbie, probably wanting to give the simplest answer possible, said, "Yes." He'd never picked up a football in his life, and I think some of the kids at school gave him a pretty hard time about it.

Bob Reagan was a strict disciplinarian, but instead of just yelling at the kids, he tried to explain to them *why* what they'd done was wrong. The funny part was, once those lectures got going, they never ended. He'd start out by saying, "Robbie, you really shouldn't talk back to your mother. You shouldn't do that because . . ." and half an hour later, "because" was still going on. Bob was a home-loving man, but he wasn't too hospitable to outsiders. My family didn't come around much, although he did enjoy the company of my cousins Velma and Kathan.

Bob loved to fish, but hunting was what he lived for. He used to go up to Maine with his buddies every year, and I think that he enjoyed the getting-ready-to-go part as much as he did the actual hunt. He'd have his clothes all organized three months ahead of time and wouldn't talk about anything else right up until it was time to leave. He loved to work in the yard, dig in the garden, and tinker in the garage or basement. If he could get his hands dirty, he was happy. He was always buying gadgets. When he died, I discovered that he had two log splitters—one wasn't enough. Also gasoline-powered drills for lumber and a cement mixer—you never can tell when you'll need one of these.

I wouldn't for one minute say it was easy being both a singer and a housewife. When I was home, Bob didn't like me to answer the telephone. He was afraid I'd say yes to some offer that was beneath me. So he would make a dive for the phone, and if it was business, screen it for me. If he decided it was OK for me to take the call, he'd yell, "Mother! Put down the mop and come to the telephone!" I didn't think it was very funny, but I tried to keep the balance as best as I could and worry as much about keeping up with the vacuuming and dusting as I did about my concert bookings.

I later found out that I wasn't the only soprano who was expected to be a good wife. Carol Fox told me a funny story about going shopping in Chicago with Elisabeth Schwarzkopf. The shop they were in had two beautiful gowns that Schwarzkopf wanted to buy, but she could only take one because her husband, the record producer Walter Legge, would be furious if she blew all that money on *two* gowns. She finally came up with the answer to her problem: She bought both and left one with Carol. The next time Schwarzkopf came through Chicago, she picked it up at Carol's house, so it looked like she'd made a separate shopping trip.

When I wasn't on the road, I kept pretty close to home—Bob and I never socialized all that much. Once in a while, though, an invitation came along that was too good to pass up. I met Rosa Ponselle for the first time when I was singing a concert in Baltimore in the early '50s. She had a party for me at Villa Pace, her spectacular home outside the city. A couple of years later, she invited us to dinner there. She was suffering from shingles, but that didn't take away from the effect she had on us. Rosa had the most natural style and glamour. She'd been the only opera star I idolized, but once I was around her, she didn't make me feel nervous or intimidated. She served leg of lamb, and she said she'd worried all day that we might not like it. (We did.) At dinner, she said, "One of the things you *must* sing is *Norma*." After we finished eating, she and I went to the piano and played through "Mira, o Norma." Her boyfriend recorded it and sent it to me later on.

Rosa and I corresponded with each other for many years after that. At the end of her life, her arthritis was so bad that she couldn't write at all, and when she sent me a Christmas card or dictated a letter, she'd press her lipstick-covered lips to a piece of paper and leave the impression for her signature. I've kept all of those notes.

⌣⌢

Without a doubt, the smartest thing I ever did as a singer was to join the Bach Aria Group. On the radio I had sung so much music, but one composer I had missed, somehow, was Bach. Then, in the early 1950s, I was asked to appear as guest soloist with the Bach Aria Group. It had been launched in 1946 by a man named William Scheide, and even though he was strictly self-taught when it came to music, he knew more about Bach than anyone I've ever met. In his library in Princeton, he had the complete *gesellschaft*. Scheide came from oil money and majored in history at Princeton, where he'd gotten interested in Beethoven's music. After he graduated, he decided to give Bach a whirl and fell in love with it; it became his life. During World War II, he'd given a lot of thought to how to launch a group dedicated to performing the great Bach vocal music. He got a bunch of musicians together, and in 1946 they gave their first concert at Bard College in Annandale-on-Hudson, New York. By the late 1940s, the Bach Aria Group was doing quite a few NBC radio broadcasts—and Scheide's idea started to take off.

In the early 1950s, Scheide decided to make some personnel changes. Norman Farrow, who'd been one of the group's original members, stayed on as bass-baritone soloist, but lots of others rotated in as guest artists. Julie Baker and Bernie Greenhouse had joined the group, and they suggested that Scheide hire me for a concert.

At first it was difficult for me to manage all that florid music—I've always said that Bach must have hated sopranos. I'd been used to singing heavier concert repertory, pieces for dramatic soprano where I could just let my voice pour out into the audience. Now, with Bach, I had to lighten my voice to keep those tricky vocal lines moving along at the right pace by concentrating even more on my breath control. Whenever I sang, I had pictures in my mind, and when I performed Bach, I imagined that my voice was floating on top of the music as I went along. If I was doing it right, it was as if I was singing "higher" than the notes—not sharp, just above them, somehow. Singing Bach, I couldn't let my voice get heavy and loud, and it couldn't go rolling out into the auditorium the way it did when I sang Wagner.

At my first concert, at Town Hall, I sang an aria from Cantata no. 14. It went well, and after the concert, when Scheide and I were on our way to a reception, I kept grabbing my throat. Scheide was a very nervous man, and he immediately thought something was wrong. "What's the matter with you?" he asked me. "Aren't you feeling well?"

"No," I said, "it feels wonderful. It's just that I can't *believe* this music! It feels so good for my voice!"

Before long, Scheide asked me to become the group's permanent soprano soloist. I accepted right away because I could tell how healthy it was for me to sing Bach—it's like doing nonstop vocalises. Singing all that lighter music kept my voice from getting too bogged down by all the Wagner and other things I was doing. It's something more singers should be careful about. If you're just singing dramatic repertory, that heaviness can creep up on you before you know it. One of today's singers I like best is Deborah Voigt. She has a gorgeous voice, but I worry about her, too. I hope she keeps Italian roles in her repertory to lighten her voice and doesn't get sucked into singing too much Wagner and Strauss.

I know Mozart cleans up your voice just as Bach does, but I never cared for Mozart—especially the opera roles, where you sing, you talk, you sing, you talk—God, it must be awful! You never get to plunge right into the music and stay there. I admire people who sing Mozart's operas, but I don't know how they do it.

The Bach Aria Group held a series of concerts at Town Hall every year, and it had a very loyal band of subscribers. You'd look out in the audience and see the same faces in the same seats, season after season. Around the time I came along, Jan Peerce joined the group as regular tenor soloist. I adored Jan. In the beginning, Scheide and some of the others were afraid that, being Jewish, Jan might not want to sing some of Bach's religious texts, but he was a complete professional and never said a word about it. Carol Smith was the alto. Throw in Julie and Bernie, the oboist, Bobby Bloom, and all the other guys in the orchestra, and it was the most terrific bunch I ever worked with. We laughed ourselves sick, but when we had to work, we were all business. My favorite part of performing with the Bach Aria Group was when we all went on tour together. We were booked into big cities and small towns. When we went out on the road, one hilarious thing happened after another. I remember how hard we used to laugh at Carol Smith. Someone would tell a dirty joke, and when Carol repeated it in Italian, it sounded twice as funny, and we'd scream like a bunch of idiots. Once, we were performing somewhere along the Gulf Coast of Florida. Carol, Julie, Bernie, and I went into a Polynesian restaurant to have dinner. The waiter brought over a big bowl of hot mustard. "Be very careful of it," he warned us. "It's very hot." "Oh, I *love* hot mustard!" Carol said, sounding very much like the prima donna. "It's so good for your sinuses! I'll sing tonight like I've never sung before!"

Julie Baker turned to me and muttered, "The minute she gets onstage, watch lightning shoot out of her ass!"

Jan Peerce was lots of fun, too. At one concert, I had finished my aria and it was Jan's turn to do his, and as I was going back to sit down, I whispered, "Your fly's open." Poor Jan spent the first few minutes of the aria constantly looking down to make sure he was zipped up. Another time, in France, Jan and Julie went to a spa. Some very prim, straitlaced-looking gal wearing glasses was passing out towels to them, and Julie nearly came apart when Jan started walking toward this woman, wearing nothing but a towel, singing, "Il est doux . . . il est bon!" from *Hérodiade*.

Julie Baker's wife, Ruth, used to leave him lists that told him which shirt and tie went with which jacket because he couldn't be trusted to figure it out for himself. We'd be out somewhere and all of a sudden Julie would say, "I have to go back to my room to find out what I'm going to wear tonight!" One time, when Julie and Bernie and I were on the outs with some of the others in the group, Julie suggested we spin off into a private ensemble of our own. We decided we'd name it after Johann Joachim Quantz, a composer who came a few years after Bach. To this day, Bernie, Julie, and I refer to ourselves as the Quantz Aria Group. These days, I don't see enough of Bernie and Julie, but recently the Quantz Aria Group had a reunion in my apartment in New Jersey, and over wine and take-out ravioli, we laughed just as much as we did forty years ago.

Bill Scheide was funny in a different way. During our concerts, his nerves would get the better of him, and he'd run around like a maniac backstage, asking all of us as we came off, "How do you think it went? What do you think?" Then, at the end, he'd come out and take a bow with the performers! I used to love to watch the faces of the people in the audience when Scheide suddenly appeared. They looked so confused. You could practically hear them asking each other, "Who is this guy? Maybe he's Bach?"

One of my favorite memories is of Scheide on tour. We would land at the airport, and he'd be so eager to get his suitcase that he'd practically throw himself on top of the luggage carousel. That was so he wouldn't have to tip a porter twenty-five cents. Even though he had family money, he was awfully tightfisted. In fact, his mother controlled the purse strings. Once, when Bernie Greenhouse wanted an advance on his salary to buy a new cello, Scheide said, "Well, I don't know—I'll have to ask Mother."

When I was in the Bach Aria Group, we were always being criticized for some of the choices we made. We'd appear in some small town where most people had never heard of Bach, and nine times out of ten, some really smart person would pipe up and say, "Why don't you use a harpsichord?" For one thing, we couldn't afford to. Since we obviously couldn't count on every little dump we played having a harpsichord, we would have had to cart it around with us, and the cost would have put us out of business in no time.

I sang so much glorious music with the Bach Aria Group. One cantata I'll always remember is no. 51, "Jauchzet Gott in allen landen!," which I did when I was seven months pregnant with Kathleen. A lot of times, we closed the first half with "Mein glaubige herz" from Cantata no. 68. Bernie Greenhouse had to start it on the cello, and he'd whisper to me, "How fast do you want it tonight?" Then he would tear into it, and we'd build speed as it went from one of us to the other—soprano, tenor, alto and bass—like a game of hot potato. Bobby Bloom, who played the oboe part that winds up the piece, would say, "Not so fast, it's going to be out of control by the time it gets to me!" "Mein glaubige herz" brought down the house every time.

In the 1960s, I went on a two-week tour of Europe with the Bach Aria Group. I took Robbie with me, and he was thrilled to be there, even though I wasn't much of a traveling companion. It was always hard for me to combine work with sight-seeing. For years, Kathleen has made fun of the movies I took of the mountains in South America while Tommy Schippers and I were there on tour—she always says that it's like a still that goes on for ten minutes. When I was with Robbie in Paris, I stayed at the bottom of the Eiffel Tower while he went all the way up. There was

Performing with the Bach Aria
Group: Bernard Greenhouse, me,
Carol Smith, Jan Peerce, Norman
Farrow. Personal collection of
Eileen Farrell.

no way I was going up there—I've always been afraid of heights. (Actually, I'm a devout coward. I'm afraid of just about everything—the water, the dark—you name it. For years I was afraid of cats, but now that Kathleen has three, I've had to get over it.)

That trip to Europe with the Bach Aria Group didn't end so well. When we were about to leave France and head for home, Scheide and some of the others held a secret meeting to discuss getting rid of Jan and me. Whenever Jan and I appeared with the group, we got our regular recital fees, which amounted to much more than anybody else in the group was paid. As time went on, Scheide felt he couldn't afford us any longer, so he fired us! I later heard that he had been planning to dump us long before we went to Europe. Jan and I thought this was a pretty slimy way to handle the whole thing, and I laid out flat the members who had been in on it. I thought we were all friends, and it was a sorry way to end a wonderful association. I think the only one who was happy with the result was Bob. He was very jealous of the time I spent on the road with the group. He knew how much fun we had, but he couldn't imagine what that music-making experience was like. Every year he'd try to talk me out of performing with them, saying it wasn't worth it, that it wasn't enough money, that it took me away from home for too many weeks of the year. Finally, he got his wish.

In 1953, I lost my father. He'd been in poor health for years: In 1946, while crossing the street in Woonsocket, he slipped on some ice and fractured his leg. At the hospital, the X-rays turned up something much, much worse: The bone was peppered with cancer. He had prostate cancer that had spread to virtually every bone by the time it was diagnosed. He was terribly sick and in and out of veterans' hospitals for the next seven years. The doctors tried all kinds of treatment to relieve his pain, but nothing worked for long. They gave him estrogen hormone treatments.

Later, they removed his testicles, and eventually, his adrenal glands. As his cancer progressed, he was particularly plagued with agonizing pain in his head and shoulders. I remember going to visit him in the Veterans' Hospital in Boston. As I got off the elevator, I heard him screaming, "Lord Jesus, please make this stop!" Finally, the only thing the doctors could do to relieve the pain was to cut the nerves in his neck. He died not long after that, on November 8, 1953. We were all relieved that his suffering had ended, but there wasn't any question that the world felt much different without him in it. It seemed unfair that someone who loved life as much as my father did should have been put through such unbearable pain at the end. As difficult as he made my mother's life from time to time, she had always loved him, and she was devastated by losing him. True to form, she tried her best not to show it.

Six and a half years later, I lost my sister, too. In 1960, just as I was about to go on tour with the Bach Aria Group, Leona called me.

"I've just come from the doctor," she said, "And I have cancer in both lungs. He's given me three months to live."

I was shocked beyond belief—Leona had never smoked a cigarette in her life. Actually, as it turned out, she had breast cancer that had metastasized to her lungs.

"I don't want Mother to know," said Leona. "And don't you tell her, either." Instead, she told my mother that she had pleurisy and was going to be hospitalized and put in an oxygen tent.

Leona was lucky; she didn't have to suffer for three months. A week and a half after she called me, she was gone. On March 7, I was in Arizona with the Bach Aria Group when I got word that she had died. I sang that evening's concert, then took a midnight plane to New York and hopped a train to Woonsocket. I got there in time for the Mass but had to skip the burial, because I was scheduled to sing another concert that night. I got there in

With my brother, John, and sister,
Leona—I sure was lucky to have
them both. Personal collection of
Eileen Farrell.

time for the second half, and it was one of the hardest performances I ever sang. I wanted to be in Rhode Island with the family, saying good-bye to my only sister. I thought of all the good
luck I'd had, how other people had taken me in hand and gotten
my career off the ground. I'd been taken care of every step of
the way, and Leona had had to struggle a half-inch at a time for
everything. What guts she had. I missed her so much at that moment, and the only thing that got me through that performance
was that I knew she'd expect it of me. That night in Arizona, I
sang my heart out for Leona.

CHAPTER EIGHT

Y 1955, MY CAREER was on a steady rise. I had all the orchestra and recital engagements I could manage. The Bach Aria Group was thriving, and as much as I loved going off on tour with that crowd, I tried never to be away from home for too long, in case my husband and children forgot what I looked like. We weren't rich, but we weren't poor, either, and it didn't bother me in the least that I wasn't a superstar. I loved what I was doing, and I was earning a good living in the process.

Then, in 1955, something unexpected came along that sped up the pace of my career. Out in Hollywood, Metro-Goldwyn-Mayer was planning to make a movie version of the soprano Marjorie Lawrence's autobiography, *Interrupted Melody*. Marjorie Lawrence had one of the greatest (and biggest) voices of her time. She'd grown up in rural Australia, and from there she'd gone on to become one of the Metropolitan Opera's biggest stars. Then in 1941, Lawrence contracted polio in Mexico City. Her paralysis was so severe that she never walked again, and most people assumed that her career was finished. But with the help of her husband, Dr. Thomas King, Lawrence made a comeback with orchestra engagements, USO tours, recordings, and eventually, opera performances that were specially staged so she could sing from a sitting position.

When *Interrupted Melody* was published in 1949, M-G-M optioned it, but it took a long time for the movie to be made. At one point it was announced for Lana Turner, and later for Greer Garson, who actually spent several months preparing for the role by studying the various opera arias to be used in the movie. But Garson left M-G-M before the movie was ready to be shot, and the part of Marjorie Lawrence went to Eleanor Parker. Eleanor had been around Hollywood for years, and her work in *The Voice of the Turtle, Caged,* and *Detective Story* had earned her quite a following. But *Interrupted Melody* was the biggest chance of her career, and she knew it. There was just one problem: Eleanor couldn't sing any better than Lana Turner or Greer Garson could.

At first, M-G-M decided that Marjorie Lawrence herself should dub the musical numbers. The studio made two complete recordings with her, but she was getting on in years, and her voice wasn't quite there anymore. She was furious when the producer, Jack Cummings, had to tell her they weren't using her vocals. At this point, my old friend Bobby Tucker got involved. I had known Bobby back at CBS. His radio show was on every weekday morning, and he was one of the best jazz pianists I knew. He left CBS around the time I did and went out to M-G-M, where he got a job in the music department.

Bobby was assigned to work on arrangements for *Interrupted Melody,* and when Marjorie Lawrence was vetoed, he suggested me for the job. I was delighted to do it, but I told them they'd have to wait a while because I was expecting Kathy. After a start date was agreed on, they sent me the music.

I sifted through the arias, and I thought, well, there's nothing here I *can't* sing, but I don't believe Marjorie Lawrence sang all of them. The selections were really all over the place. The Immolation Scene and the *Tristan* Liebestod—fine. But "Un bel dì"? Musetta's Waltz? And "Mon coeur s'ouvre à ta voix" from *Samson et Dalila,* which eventually was used as a recurring theme in the picture? Dalila is almost a contralto part, and I knew Lawrence hadn't gone near *that* one. But this was Hollywood, and M-G-M wanted certain pieces of music in the picture, whether or not they made sense. I decided to keep my mouth shut.

When I flew out to California, I stayed with Bobby and Johnny Payne (no relation to the actor John Payne). They had a place not far from M-G-M, and John dropped Bobby and me at the studio every morning. Most of the time, I was scheduled to work with Walter DuCloux, a sweetheart of a man who was a staff conductor for the fabulous M-G-M orchestra. I recorded the arias on a huge soundstage, and though a full month had been allotted to complete the recordings, we finished in two and a half weeks. Eleanor Parker dropped by the sessions several times. She was filming *Many Rivers to Cross,* with Robert Taylor, and she'd show up in her pioneer-gal costume from that picture and go right into the control room to watch me. Knowing this was the best role she'd ever had, Eleanor practically drove herself to a nervous breakdown preparing for it. In a lot of old Hollywood movies, the lip-synching was pretty sloppy, and Eleanor wanted hers to be completely convincing. The engineers put a beep on her recordings right before she was supposed to take a breath, so it would look like she really knew what she was doing when it came to breath support.

I didn't worry about trying to sound like Marjorie Lawrence, and just sang everything in the picture in my natural voice. The only spot where I really had to do any "acting" was in the scene in Mexico City where she first becomes ill while rehearsing *Tris-*

tan; I had to show that in my voice. Otherwise, it was a breeze. The engineers were thrilled with how smoothly everything went. "You can't imagine how many individual notes we have to save," one of them told me, "because the singer happens to like the notes." He told me about a famous movie soprano recording a number for a certain picture, and how she sat next to him for days listening to the tapes over and over, telling him, "Now take that note from the first take and those notes from the fourth take . . ." "With you," said the engineer, "we can use the complete take."

The people I worked with at M-G-M were very congenial, especially Johnny Green, head of the music department, and the picture's music supervisor, Saul Chaplin. Since I was singing all day, I didn't have much time for Hollywood parties, but I did get to know Mitzi Gaynor and her wonderful husband, Jack Bean, and Keenan Wynn, who were all friends of Bobby and Johnny's. Helen Traubel was on the lot, filming *Deep in My Heart* with Jose Ferrer, and we ran into each other several times.

I saw the finished film of *Interrupted Melody* for the first time in a screening room at M-G-M. George Trovillo was with me, and as I sat there watching Eleanor Parker do a perfect job of lip-synching, I actually managed to forget that it was really my voice coming out of her. When I took my mother to the premiere at Radio City Music Hall, it was one of the few times she really seemed impressed with something I'd done. As the end credits rolled, she said over and over, "Beautiful . . . it's just beautiful." *Interrupted Melody* was a huge success for M-G-M and for Eleanor Parker, who got an Academy Award nomination for Best Actress of 1955.

When I signed the contract to do the picture, I was given two options: Either I could receive screen credit, which would give me a certain amount of money, or I could waive screen credit, which would give me more money. Easiest decision I ever made. My name went out on the soundtrack recording, which was a big seller. It might as well have been on the screen, too, because M-G-M mentioned me in the studio press releases, so all the newspaper critics and columnists wrote that it was my voice in the picture. I got a lot of attention, reaching a wider audience than I'd ever imagined, and my stock went up quite a bit. At the time, though, all *Interrupted Melody* really meant to me was that I could afford to walk into The Tailored Woman on Fifty-seventh Street and Fifth Avenue, breeze past all the stuffy clerks, and pick out the most expensive mink coat I could lay my hands on.

As time went on, I never got over the thrill of meeting people I'd idolized, and one of them was Judy Garland. I was checking into the Plaza Hotel in Manhattan, where I would stay for a week while rehearsing for some concerts with Lenny Bernstein and the New York Philharmonic. All of a sudden Judy Garland stepped up to the desk to check her messages. I wasn't about to let this opportunity pass by.

"Excuse me," I said, "I just wanted to say hello. I'm Eileen Farrell."

Judy's mouth flew open and she gave me a big smile and grabbed me by the arm. "Of *course* you are!" she said, and steered me over to a sofa in the lobby. We sat there and talked about this and that for nearly an hour, while people walked by staring at us. I told her about that night's concert, and she told me she'd be sure to come. Sure enough, she did, with Jule Styne as her date. There was a dinner after the concert, and Judy sat at my table, and we talked about absolutely everything. She told me that she hated to have formal photos taken, and whenever she had to sit for portraits, she insisted that they play my records for her; she claimed it relaxed her and put her in a good mood. Judy was just marvelous company that night. She must have been awfully lonely; she had a knack for making you feel you were going to be best friends forever. But, in fact, I never saw her again.

Another time—I think it was in the early '50s—I sang for a special luncheon at the Waldorf-Astoria honoring the violinist Fritz Kreisler. I sang a couple of arias and after the luncheon was finished, I got on the elevator and saw Helen Keller standing there. Her companion signed to her that I had just gotten on the elevator. Miss Keller reached out and put her hand on my throat and held it there for a minute. Her companion explained that while I was singing at the luncheon, Miss Keller had put her hand on the top of the table and "heard" my voice by feeling the vibrations.

By the midfifties, I was still appearing on a few radio programs, mostly *The Bell Telephone Hour* and *The Railroad Hour,* but television had taken over. For several years, live concerts and recitals had been my bread and butter, but since many of the radio musicians I once worked with had moved into television, I didn't see why I shouldn't do the same. Variety shows were all over the place, and many of them weren't afraid of programming classical music.

One singer who got tremendous exposure on television was Helen Traubel. She'd been singing Wagner at the Met since the early 1940s, but she had a yen to sing pop tunes, which she frequently did in nightclubs and TV variety programs. One of her most famous numbers was "The Song's Gotta Come from the Heart," which she recorded with Jimmy Durante. I'm not saying that pop music suited Helen very well; she may have loved it, but she didn't have a real flair for it, and she usually came across as a grand lady slumming.

I'd been dying to sing pop songs in public ever since I had started doing "He Was Too Good to Me" on the party circuit back in the midforties. I didn't do them on my recital programs, because singers just didn't mix it up the way they do now, with the rise of what has come to be known as "crossover." (This has got to be one of the stupidest words ever invented. I really don't have the faintest idea what it means. A few years ago, when *Opera News* magazine ran a profile of me, they called me the "Queen of Crossover," and at first I had no idea what they were talking about.)

Recital programs were carefully organized, beginning with, say, a couple of arias, then a group of German, French, and English songs. Even on my early TV appearances—*The Colgate Comedy Hour* and Milton Berle's *Texaco Star Theater*—I'd just come out and sing an aria. From the start, though, I loved doing television. Under a tight deadline, everyone pulls together to get the show in shape for that week's telecast. In all my years on TV, there were far fewer ego trips than I later found on the opera stage. Apart from everything else, there just wasn't time.

One of the programs I performed on many times was *The Ed Sullivan Show* on CBS. Doing the Sullivan show was always like going home, because it was filmed at the same theater where I'd done a lot of my radio shows in the '40s. The pace was brisk on any TV variety show, but *Ed Sullivan* was especially crazy. It was broadcast live, and all my activity was confined to the one day the show aired, Sunday. I would arrive at 8 A.M. for a blocking rehearsal. In the afternoon, we would hold a dress rehearsal, which was taped. Ed Sullivan would watch the tape between dress rehearsal and air time and decide if he wanted anything changed. That night, we'd go live on the air. The Sullivan show was filmed with a standard three-camera setup: I'd hit my marks, and when the red light went on, I was on camera and it was time to deliver.

The Ed Sullivan Show was one of the top-rated shows on TV because of the quality and diversity of the guest stars, but Ed Sullivan's personal success had to be one of the strangest show business stories ever. He was an odd man, and offstage he was a lot like he appeared on the tube—stiff, awkward, and humorless. I think in truth he was probably very shy. But he respected talent,

As Isolde on *The Bell Telephone Hour.*
Courtesy of NBC-TV.

and loved showcasing it every week, even though some of his choices were a little strange—Jerry Vale, who wasn't much, was on all the time just because his wife was friendly with Sylvia Sullivan (Ed's wife).

I don't think Ed cared much about classical music, and probably even less for opera, but he believed it had a place on his show. On the very first telecast of *Toast of the Town* back in 1948, the pianist Eugene List, who'd played for Stalin and Churchill at Potsdam, was one of the guests. In 1956, Sullivan presented the Metropolitan Opera in extended scenes, including Maria Callas in *Tosca,* over several weeks. He took a beating in the ratings because of it, but he still kept opera stars on the schedule. After the failure of the Met series, there were no more complete scenes, only four-minute arias. If you chose an aria that was longer than four minutes, you had to cut it to fit.

Like most variety-show hosts, Sullivan depended on cue cards, which gave him no end of trouble. Once he introduced a guest as being a veteran of "World War i . . . i." One of his most frequent opera guests was my pal Robert Merrill, who always helped Sullivan write out the names of the arias phonetically. It didn't do much good; once Ed paid Bob back by announcing, "I'd like to prevent Robert Merrill." Roberta Peters was on his show a lot, and more than once he introduced her as Roberta Sherwood, a pop singer of the time. In fact, I think the only names he ever got right were Señor Wences and Topo Gigiot, the sidekicks he had on every week. I got off more easily than most, but one night he introduced me as "Eileen O'Farrell." Still, I do have Ed Sullivan to thank for audiences getting to know me as a pop singer.

In the summer of 1959 I was booked for my first performances in Europe. I was to begin with a concert at Royal Albert Hall in London, then repeat the program at Milan's La Scala, finishing up at the second annual Spoleto Festival, where I would also perform the Verdi Requiem, with Tommy Schippers conducting.

The Albert Hall performance went well, and while I was in London, I had lunch at the Savoy with Ruth O'Neill and Bill Judd of the concert bureau Judson, O'Neill and Judd, who had become my agents after Horace Parmelee's death. We were just getting settled, when we noticed a small table for two with a reserved sign on it a short distance away. Maria Callas was in London at the time, rehearsing *Medea*. "That's probably Callas's table," joked Bill Judd, and he'd hardly gotten the words out of his mouth when she walked in and sat down at that table. I sat there thinking, God—I'm so nearsighted; maybe she's looking at me and maybe she isn't. But I certainly could not ignore her, so I excused myself and went over to her table.

"Miss Callas," I said, "I'm sorry to interrupt your lunch, but I just wanted to introduce myself. I'm Eileen Farrell."

I was half-expecting her to say, "Who the hell cares?" Instead, she jumped to her feet and threw her arms around me.

"It's wonderful to see you," she said. "Are you staying in London long?"

I told her I was about to leave for Milan and Spoleto.

"How long will you be in Italy?" she asked. "Because I'm not using my house there, and I would love for you to use it for as long as you'd like."

I thanked her and told her I'd be spending most of my time in Spoleto, which was out of the way. But we sat there and talked, like old friends, for several more minutes. Then I went back to my table. After Ruth and Bill and I finished lunch, we passed by Callas on the way out of the restaurant. I was just going to smile and not bother her, but she stood up again, put her arms around me, and said, "I want you to know that of all my colleagues, you have been the nicest to me." I was on the verge of tears as I stumbled out of the Savoy.

Van Cliburn was appearing in London at the time, and he was also managed by Ruth O'Neill and Bill Judd. Ruth and Bill had to go from London to Amsterdam on business, and since Van and I had some breathing room in our schedules, we decided to go with them. We had no idea what we were in for. Amsterdam was hosting the Holland Music Festival, during which everyone pilots boats through the fabulous canals. When the festival manager found out that Van and I were there, he put a grand piano on a giant barge and sent us floating off into the night. All the glorious Dutch houses were lit up as we cruised down the canals. It was cold, but that didn't stop Van and me from drinking and singing and whooping it up into the wee hours. The next morning I woke up and found out that the night air had worked its magic. I couldn't speak a word.

I had to cancel my La Scala recital, which turned out to be my one and only chance to sing there. From Amsterdam I flew to Rome to spend a few days at the Hassler Hotel before driving up to Spoleto.

It was only the second year of the Spoleto Festival, so it didn't resemble the institution it is today, and the town was unspoiled, to say the least. There were very few shops, and although I loved the accommodations, they were on the rustic side. If you wanted to use the bathroom, you had to line up in the hall. The owner of the hotel parked himself at the entrance, so he could watch everyone going in and out. He gave you the heave-ho if you didn't belong and screamed at his staff if they so much as looked like they were about to make a mistake.

For the opening night of the festival, the glitterati came up by train from Rome, all in the gorgeous Italian fashions. The first thing I did was my recital with Tommy, which gave me my first experience with music-loving Italians; right in the middle of one of my songs, they all started to stomp their feet and cheer. The next day, as I was making my way up the narrow little street that led to the hotel, people leaned out their windows and shouted, "BRAVA DIVA!"

The festival had quite a lineup that season: Sir John Gielgud was giving dramatic readings, and Louis Armstrong was scheduled to give a concert with his band. Ed Sullivan was there, too, because he'd decided he would telecast from Spoleto, showing festival highlights, to replace the usual summer reruns. This kind of thing was practically unheard of at the time, and it took a lot of guts and ingenuity on the part of the Sullivan team. Sullivan wanted to film me singing "Pace, pace" with Tommy playing in the Greek Theater, an ancient amphitheater. The only entrance was through a tiny door at the bottom, and the grand piano had to be wedged through the door and hoisted up on pulleys to get it to the spot they had settled on. They had a hard time positioning the cameras where they wanted them, so "Pace, pace" was filmed at a medium-to-long distance. Once that segment was shot, I assumed that my commitment to the Sullivan show was completed.

Tommy and I were rehearsing the Verdi Requiem, which was not scheduled to be part of the telecast, when Sullivan came running up frantically and asked us to stop. It seemed that Louis Armstrong, who was supposed to film a number for Ed, had gotten pneumonia while staying in Yester House, Gian Carlo Menotti's drafty old estate in Scotland. Ed needed a last-minute replacement. "I know you can sing pop music, because you used to do it at parties," he said. "Would you save our necks and sing 'On the Sunny Side of the Street'?"

What could I say? Because everything was being shot outside, where the sound quality would be iffy, I would have to lip-synch to a playback. We recorded the song in a tiny nightclub on the second floor of some old building. When it came time to tape the show, I mouthed the words while Louis Armstrong's band accompanied me. I had a fabulous time, and the band paid me its ultimate tribute in jazz lingo, by calling me "solid." Both audiences and the press went wild over my "transformation" from classical soprano to pop singer. I didn't realize it yet, but I had taken the first step in a major new phase of my career, and I had Ed Sullivan to thank for it.

The Spoleto performance was a hot news item, and Bill Judd knew it, so he telephoned one of the best press representatives in the business, Edgar Vincent, to see if Edgar could get some mileage out of it. Did he ever—stories about the concert diva who could sing jazz popped up in newspapers and magazines everywhere. Edgar handled press for me for many years. In 1961, he even got me on the cover of *Newsweek.* Editors seemed to love the fact that I was a housewife as well as a singer, and that I was married to a New York cop. There was a lot of diva-at-home-on-Staten-Island stuff. Once, *The New York Times* even published a bunch of my recipes, including "Filet of Sole Eileen Farrell." I remember that it had mandarin oranges in it—well, what do you want? It was the '60s, for God's sake.

Some time before, I had signed an exclusive recording contract with Columbia Records, and we had a couple of big ones in the can—*Eileen Farrell Sings Puccini Arias,* with Max Rudolf conducting the Columbia Symphony, and a recital of Schubert, Schumann, Debussy, and Poulenc songs, with George Trovillo at the piano. Goddard Lieberson, the president of Columbia Masterworks, and his right-hand man, Schuyler Chapin, got the idea that I should capitalize on my Spoleto success by cutting a record of blues songs. They hired Luther Henderson as conductor and arranger, and I sang sizzling versions of "Blues in the Night," "Glad to Be Unhappy," "He Was Too Good to Me," "Ten Cents a Dance" and several others—including "I've Got a Right to Sing the Blues," which became the title cut.

I was thrilled with the results, but Columbia was puzzled about how to release all these albums. They were afraid they

With members of Louis Armstrong's
band, singing "Sunny Side of the
Street," Spoleto, Italy, 1959. It was
such a hit that it led to a second
career as a pop singer. Courtesy of
Opera News.

might cancel each other out and decided it would be best to put a distance of several months between the release dates. Then my old friend Mitch Miller, who had since become a famous band-leader and happened to be on Columbia's board of directors, came up with a savvy marketing plan: Why not release all three albums simultaneously? This way, Columbia could give a complete profile of an unusual voice, and the sales of each of the three disks would probably increase the demand for the other two.

And that's exactly what happened. All three records sold well, but *I've Got a Right to Sing the Blues* really went over the top. It was a best-seller on the pop charts for weeks and eventually led to a sequel LP with Luther, *Here I Go Again,* in which we took on "Somebody Loves Me," "The Second Time Around," "Wrap Your Troubles in Dreams," and many others. People kept writing about the "two voices" of Eileen Farrell, but I didn't look at it that way. Singing pop or arias requires the same basic technique of breath control, diction, and knowing what the hell you're singing about, but using a different style for each. The ability to feel at home in different styles doesn't come to everybody. Either you've got it or you don't, and most opera singers don't. The demands of good pop singing—the phrasing, rhythmic flexibility, the ability to tell a story in song—seems to escape them. I recently saw Kiri Te Kanawa make hash out of "Why Don't You Do Right?" on public television. (The bass player was telling her how to phrase as she sang it!) The most beautiful voice in the world doesn't necessarily make you a good pop singer. You have to understand the words and get them across; you have to feel the underbeat. In my day, Dorothy Kirsten and Risë Stevens could handle a pop song, and Patrice Munsel wasn't bad. Most of the others were out in left field. I've given up listening to today's opera stars who try to sing pop. I can only say that I don't like any of the ones I've heard.

When it came to pop songwriters, I favored Rodgers and

With Luther Henderson at a
recording session for my first album
of pop standards, *I've Got a Right to
Sing the Blues*. Courtesy Angel
Records.

Hart and Harold Arlen. I never knew Larry Hart, but I was lucky enough to know both Dick Rodgers and Harold Arlen. Over the years, I would run into Dick at parties, and in 1965, at a memorial service for Adlai Stevenson, Dick accompanied me while I sang "You'll Never Walk Alone." By the time we were finished, there wasn't a dry seat in the house.

For me, the songs Dick composed when he worked with Larry Hart had a snap and vitality and passion that were missing in his collaborations with Oscar Hammerstein. Larry Hart and Oscar Hammerstein were totally different kinds of lyricists, of course, but Hart's words always seemed so real and true, while Hammerstein's seemed, I don't know . . . a little stagey. I think Alec Wilder hit it on the head about Hammerstein in his wonderful book, *American Popular Song:* "I have always felt that there was an almost feverish demand in Hart's writing which reflected itself in Rodgers' melodies as opposed to the almost too comfortable armchair philosophy in Hammerstein's lyrics."

I was always crazy about Harold Arlen. Harold grew up with music; he was the son of a cantor, and later he played piano, sang in nightclubs, and worked as a dance-band arranger. Harold's songs are completely singable, and always feel just right for my voice. Cole Porter wrote wonderful lyrics, but I didn't feel his sophisticated New York edge really suited me, and I sang very few of his songs. I admire Irving Berlin (his "Always" was my first single for Decca, back in the '40s), but a lot of his numbers are a little too corny for me. As for Gershwin, I adore *Porgy and Bess.* It was the very first complete score I ever bought when I first came to New York, and I used to perform "Summertime," "Strawberry Woman," and "I Loves You, Porgy" as encores during my recitals. As for the other songs, " 'S Wonderful" and all that . . . I don't know. I find most of Gershwin a little too upbeat, and I don't think of myself as an upbeat singer. He was a marvelous composer—I just don't think most of his songs are for me.

Lots of people have asked me over the years why I can sing pop, while so many other classically trained singers can't. I have the same answer every time: It's like dowsing. I can take a forked stick, walk through a field holding it straight out in front of me and tell you exactly the spot where a well should be dug. There's a sensation that comes through the stick and into my hands the minute I'm standing near underground water. My husband couldn't do it, and neither can my children. I can't explain it. It's just there, and I think it's the same way with pop singing.

After *I've Got a Right to Sing the Blues* was released, Birgit Nilsson called Edgar Vincent, who was now acting as press representative for both of us. "I just listened to Eileen Farrell's new album," she said. "And I'd just like to say, *I've* got a right to sing Wagner."

After I became established as a pop singer, Ed Sullivan asked me back several times. I would always sing an aria and a pop tune. Shortly after *I've Got a Right to Sing the Blues* started climbing the charts, I was booked on Ed's show and planned to sing one of the songs from the new album. After Ed watched the tape of the dress rehearsal, he decided he didn't like the song. That left about two and a half hours to go until air time. I came up with a substitute song that Ed approved, and there was a big scramble to get the orchestration from Luther Henderson. We finally got our hands on it, sped through a rehearsal with the orchestra, and went on the air. Ed got my name right this time, and then announced that I would be singing the original number he'd vetoed just three hours earlier. The camera's red light went on, and I didn't have a clue which song I was supposed to sing. Fortunately, I figured it out from the orchestra's introduction, but my blood pressure went through the roof. I had a contract for several more Sullivan shows, but after I walked off the stage that night, I was so mad that I called Bill Judd and told him to cancel them all.

I always made space on my schedule for television appearances, and the show I probably appeared on most often was *The Garry Moore Show.* The arrangements were very laid-back. Garry would call me three or four weeks ahead of taping and say, "Hey, Eileen—can you come and sing for us next month?" Garry was one of the nicest men in show business, and I adored his sidekick, Durward Kirby, and the incredible regulars—Carol Burnett, Dorothy Loudon, and Marion Lorne (who seemed every bit as batty in person as she did playing Aunt Clara on *Bewitched*). On most programs, I just stood before the cameras and sang, but on Garry's show, I often did a big, splashy production number. The one I remember best is a medley of New York songs that Ken and Mitzi Welch, Garry's special material writers, put together for Dorothy Loudon and me. It was one of the best things I ever did on TV. Dorothy and I wore black gowns and, leaning against a pair of big blue NYPD dividers, we opened with Lenny Bernstein's "New York, New York," then segued into a bunch of other New York songs. It came off beautifully. Another time, Carol Burnett and I did a big song-and-dance number in which we played two charwomen. Carol liked it so much that she made the charwoman her signature sketch when she got her own CBS show years later.

I loved Carol, and when she got a show of her own, she invited Marilyn Horne and me to join her for a pair of episodes. On one program we did a takeoff on opera buffa, called *Chinderella,* with Carol in the lead role, Harvey Korman as the Fairy Godfather, and Jackie Horne and me as the two wicked stepsisters. Another time, Carol, Jackie, and I played the Three Little Pigs, with Harvey as the Big Bad Wolf.

Carol was always serious about her work. Even though she sounded confident when she sang, she couldn't read a note of music. On her scores, she'd have little arrows written in over the words telling her whether to go up or down.

With Carol Burnett on *The Garry Moore Show*. Carol and I played charwomen in this production number, and Carol liked the character so much that it later became her signature sketch on her own show. Courtesy CBS Television.

We rehearsed Carol's show Monday through Thursday and taped on Friday. On one show, in which Carol, Jackie, and I were supposed to team up to do "Big Spender," one of Jackie's contact lenses suddenly dislodged, rattling her momentarily. She wanted to reshoot the whole number, but Joe Hamilton, Carol's husband and executive producer, explained to her that the show's schedule and budget made that impossible. Jackie and Joe had quite an argument, which put an end to the possibility of another show featuring the three of us.

I loved doing Carol's show. Like Garry Moore, she had a staff of marvelous special material writers (including Ken and Mitzi Welch). *Chinderella* was a good example of what they could do. Harry Zimmerman, Artie Malvin, and Dick De Benedictis put together an opera pastiche loaded with rich musical details and in-jokes, which they just assumed the audience would get. But this was in 1971. I'm not sure you could pull it off today.

Between the late '50s and early '70s I did a lot of other shows, too, including Al Hirt's, Danny Kaye's, Jonathan Winters's, and Jimmy Dean's (which Bob hated to have me do because Jimmy Dean had the foulest mouth in show business). From the mid-sixties on, I also did the talk shows: Merv Griffin, Virginia Graham, and Mike Douglas. Appearing on variety shows meant good money, but the trouble with talk shows was that even though they were useful for plugging your latest recording or upcoming opera appearances, they paid scale—$200. I saw no reason why I should bust my ass under the circumstances, and my agents always made it clear to Mike, Merv, and the others that Miss Farrell would talk, but Miss Farrell would not sing. Once, I was on *The Mike Douglas Show,* with my friend Kaye Ballard as cohost. We were all sitting around in a semicircle having a pleasant time, when all of a sudden Mike said, "So, Eileen—what are you going to sing for us today?"

I looked at him and said, "Oh, no, you don't."

Thank God—a break from opera:
with Dorothy Loudon, again on *The
Garry Moore Show.* Photograph by
J. Peter Happel Photography,
courtesy of CBS Television.

"What do you mean, no?"

"I told you I'm not singing."

"Oh, but you were just kidding, weren't you? I'm sure everyone watching would *love* to hear you sing."

This was a bit much—pressuring me in front of a television audience to perform! Needless to say, it was my swan song on *The Mike Douglas Show.*

I don't know when they started, but over time, a lot of stories about me started making the rounds. The point of most of them was that I supposedly had the foulest mouth in show business. Now, I'm not saying I didn't. At home, when our boxers, Brandy and Sherry, were tearing around the house, more than once I yelled, "Somebody get the goddamned dogs the hell out of here!" Normal stuff like that. Sometimes I went a little bit further. Let's put it this way—I was no Helen Hayes.

Once, while I was singing with the Bach Aria Group, William Scheide called us together for the unveiling of a special portrait of Bach that he'd gotten. He was so proud of it. We were all summoned for the unveiling, and when he pulled the string, there appeared a very nice portrait of the master. All I could think of was how hard it was to learn all those damned arias, and I said, a little too loudly, "Well, if it isn't old Shitface!" Julie Baker and Bernie Greenhouse nearly stopped breathing. That one's true.

The most famous story about my mouth involves Tommy Schippers. Supposedly, we were rehearsing together, and we got in a disagreement over tempo. The story goes that I said to Tommy, "You leave the singing to me and I'll leave the c——s———g to you." Sorry—it never happened. That word is definitely *not* my style. (Once, at a rehearsal with Tommy, I did say, "It looks like Pippers is in the shit again," but that was just a joke—no malice intended.)

The peak years of my career were from the midfifties to the late sixties. It all really got rolling in 1955. It was a great year for me. The movie *Interrupted Melody* brought me a lot of attention, but the real turning point came when I was engaged by the American Opera Society to sing concert performances of Cherubini's *Medea* at Town Hall. Up until then, I had never considered singing opera because the stage direction, lighting, costumes, and cues all sounded like too much trouble—and I didn't exactly think I had the figure for the opera stage.

The American Opera Society, founded by Alan Sven Oxenburg, presented concert versions of operas that were not quite in the standard repertory. Oxenburg was famous for his casting ability. He had a knack for finding just the right singers for his operas, and he also liked to engage those of us who hadn't been overexposed at the Met and other big companies. *Medea* wasn't completely forgotten, because Maria Callas had made a big splash just two years earlier when it was revived for her in Italy—but the Town Hall concert was going to be *Medea*'s U.S. premiere.

Oxenburg was an annoying nitpicker, always looking over my shoulder and fiddling with little musical details, but he was committed to getting an excellent performance onstage, and he'd had great results. The American Opera Society's performances were eagerly awaited by New York concertgoers, and they were usually sold to the rafters. *Medea* was no exception. Arnold Gamson was the conductor, and although we made quite a few cuts, it was still an awfully demanding part.

The reviews went on and on about how difficult the music was, but I've sung many things that were much harder than *Medea*. Actually, it wasn't so hard on the voice as it was on the feet, since Medea is onstage for practically every moment of the opera. Of course, it was a challenge to get her pent-up rage and obsession with vengeance across to the audience. Alan Oxenburg lectured me for hours on end about various approaches to the character. He treated me to a little seminar on Greek mythology, telling me every twist and turn of the story of Jason and Medea, how she'd helped him capture the Golden Fleece and been struck by Cupid's arrow, and when Jason didn't need her anymore, he'd thrown her over. None of this interested me much. "That's nice, Alan," I would say, and he'd move on to the next part of his little lecture. Finally, when he realized he wasn't getting through to me with all the mythological details, he said, "She's a *bitch*." I took a black pen and very carefully wrote "BITCH" in big block letters on top of my score. After that, I understood exactly what to do, and Mr. Oxenburg didn't bother me anymore.

I thought *Medea* would be just another engagement, but it was much more than that. On opening night, Maria Callas and Zinka Milanov were in the audience, along with most of the big movers in the music business. At the end of the performance, everyone went nuts. I lost track of the curtain calls. People were leaning over the balcony, screaming and cheering. The press went nuts, too. In a profile he wrote for *The New Yorker* in 1958, Winthrop Sargeant wrote,

> Miss Farrell's voice seemed limitless in power, magnificent in tone, remarkably sure in its command of the classical style, and accurate enough to cope successfully with any of the taxing coloratura phrases that occur so frequently in *Medea* and other Italian operas of the late eighteenth and early nineteenth centuries. Inevitably, in the days that followed the performance, comparisons with better-known opera singers were drawn, since comparisons are part of the ritual observed by every entrapped opera buff. Just at that time indeed, an unofficial contest that was widely publicized as "the battle of the sopranos" was going on, the favored gladiators being Renata Tebaldi, Zinka Milanov and Maria Meneghini Callas.

It is, of course, risky to judge any singer by a single role, but of one thing Miss Farrell's listeners are sure: considered simply as a singer—without regard to such things as repertoire, stagecraft and experience—she was superior to all three. She was more consistently accurate than Miss Milanov; she had a more resonant voice, with a more limpid and pleasing quality, than Miss Callas; and, purely as a vocalist, she far outclassed the unquestionably charming Miss Tebaldi. Moreover, her lung power seemed comparable to that of the illustrious Kirsten Flagstad, and she had an elasticity of voice that Miss Flagstad, at least in her great Wagnerian days, did not possess.

The only thing that bothered me about the reaction to *Medea* was that I was being treated like an overnight discovery. For God's sake, I'd been singing in New York since 1940! Immediately, all the critics and columnists started writing that I should have been singing opera all along, that every opera company should hurry to sign me up. I resented this, in a way. I was very proud of my accomplishments on radio and the concert stage, and I didn't like the idea of those years being dismissed as if they'd never happened at all.

Columbia wanted to put the *Medea* on record. In the end, we did excerpts only, and it turned out well. But what I really remember is the photo for the album cover. Columbia decided to go all out and hire the famous Chicago dress designer Charles James to make a gown for me. He came to New York, and Bob and I met him at his hotel off Madison Avenue. He took my measurements, and three weeks later he scheduled me for a fitting. He showed up with an elaborate, uncomfortable corset. He was trying to get the corset in exactly the right position, and at one point he said, "Now, hold it right there, while I distribute the fat!" He almost got it in the groin right then and there. Two

The Medea look. Courtesy of
Angel Records.

more weeks went by, and he returned to New York with the completed costume. When he pulled it out of the boxes, we saw the hoop skirt. Bob was there, and so was my publicist, Edgar Vincent, and nobody said a word. Finally, I said, "I hate to tell you this, but Medea did not wear hoop skirts."

"Medea?" Charles James pulled himself up very straight. "Medea? This is a costume for *Medea?* I thought it was supposed to be for *Medusa.*"

I didn't know then, and I still don't know, why he thought Medusa would wear a hoop skirt, either. I thanked him for his efforts and took the costume home to Staten Island and stashed it in the back of the big wardrobe closet I had built on the third floor of our house.

Thanks to *Medea,* I was now a "new" star. I was expected to go full-throttle into opera, which I wasn't at all sure I wanted to do. I wasn't sure about the star business, either, and the effect it might have on my home life. But Columbia and Edgar Vincent were putting a lot of important career-making machinery in motion, so I decided to go along for the ride and see what would happen.

CHAPTER NINE

Y MANAGERS had gotten it into their heads that I would never be a really big star unless I did opera, and right after *Medea,* Arnold Gamson asked me which other opera roles I knew. "Not any, really," I said. He was furious but determined to set me up with a fully staged performance somewhere. I agreed on condition that my first stage performance would be somewhere out of the way.

It was eventually decided that my official opera debut would take place in 1956 in Tampa, Florida, where I would sing the role of Santuzza in *Cavalleria rusticana.* We did a few rehearsals in New York, then took off for Florida. I flew ahead of the orchestra and most of the rest of the company, and there was a terrible storm along the way. The plane carrying the orchestra was delayed for several hours, and they barely made it to the theater by curtain time. That meant not one minute of stage rehearsal for my debut, and I was scared to death.

The performances in Tampa turned out all right, and a few months later I made my debut with the San Francisco Opera as

Leonora in *Il trovatore*. San Francisco, of course, was a major company, and I knew things would run much more smoothly there. Jussi Björling was Manrico, and the conductor was Olivero de Fabritiis. I was in awe of Björling—I would get so caught up listening to the gorgeous sounds that came out of his throat that I would forget to sing! My colleagues in the concert world had for the most part been fairly easy to get along with, but it didn't take me long to figure out that in the opera world, tenors don't have to play by the rules. At the *Trovatore* dress rehearsal, Björling sang in street clothes because he'd done the part so many times by then. Before we got to the final scene, he got in a scrape with de Fabritiis, and stormed off the stage.

On the night of the performance, I had to guess which way he was going to move for the entire scene. Afterward I sat in my dressing room, taking off my makeup, thinking about how good I'd had it when I was singing concerts. No fussy costumes, no tenors who don't want to rehearse, no worrying whether I was standing in the right spot for the light to hit me. There was a lot of pressure to master Italian, too, which I had never really done before. I had simply learned individual arias and songs and coached them with various people. In opera, though, you were expected, and rightly so, to have total command of the language—or as close as you could get. So I sat down and started learning to conjugate irregular Italian verbs. It wasn't so bad. There were only 17,852 of them.

Some people thought my voice was too heavy for Leonora, but I liked singing the part, even though she was kind of a nothing character. I also did *Medea* with the San Francisco Opera, and the dual part of the Prima Donna and Ariadne in Strauss's *Ariadne auf Naxos*. I did *Ariadne* for several other companies after that. One of them would want the *vorspiel* in English and the opera itself in German, then the next company would reverse it. I still don't understand why these companies couldn't give the singers a break by all managing to get on the same page—literally. But San Francisco audiences and critics seemed to love me in opera. After one of my performances there, Alfred Frankenstein, writing in the *San Francisco Chronicle,* wrote, "Miss Farrell has a voice like some unparalleled phenomenon of nature. She is to singers what Niagara is to waterfalls." That line caught on and was used in my publicity materials and tossed around by the press for years.

I did a few operas in Chicago, too, and soon reporters started asking me why I wasn't appearing at the Met. After all, I'd had my own radio show for seven years, I'd had terrific success in the concert arena, in movies, and on TV, had a big recording contract with Columbia, and sung opera in San Francisco and Chicago. So what was the Met waiting for? It never occurred to me that I was a failure because the Met hadn't called me, so I was lucky I had the press there to remind me. For a long time, when people asked why I wasn't at the Met, I gave the same pat answer— "Nobody's asked me." The press wouldn't let it drop, though, and they started asking the Met's general manager, Rudolf Bing, about it. I'm sure he got as sick of the question as I did.

Then, in 1959, Bing made front-page headlines by firing Maria Callas from the Met. It wasn't a secret that Callas had been none too happy with her Met appearances ever since her debut in 1956. They stuck her in moldy old productions and never gave her what she considered a proper amount of rehearsal time. I had seen Callas at the Met in a performance of *Lucia di Lammermoor,* and it seemed to be an off-night for her. Maybe it was a result of the things she complained about in the press. She was no ordinary performer, and she needed good productions and good directors in order to show off what she did best.

In the middle of all this furor over Callas getting axed, I got an unexpected load of publicity. A reporter asked Callas about the whole flap with Bing, and she answered, "Who needs the Met? They don't have any big names. They haven't got Farrell,

Rehearsing with Carlo Felice
Cillario, Lyric Opera of Chicago.
Photograph by Nancy Sorenson,
courtesy of Lyric Opera of Chicago.

have they?" This really sent the press to working overtime on my behalf. Then Max Rudolf, who had conducted me in a Puccini album released around this time, went to Bing and said, "You can't possibly delay inviting her to the Met. This is one of the major voices of our time." Finally, I guess Bing had no choice but to give in. One day, when I was at home on Staten Island, the phone rang.

"Hello, Miss Farrell," said the voice on the other end. "This is Mr. Bing of the Metropolitan Opera."

I remembered the story I'd heard about Bing calling Bert Lahr in the early 1950s to ask him to appear in the Met production of *Die Fledermaus*.

"Hello, Mr. Lahr. This is Mr. Bing."

"Oh, hello, Mr. *Bing!* This is Mr. *Bang!*"

"No, Mr. Lahr. This really *is* Mr. Bing of the Metropolitan Opera."

The two of them kept this up for several minutes before Bert figured out that it really wasn't a joke. (Most of us learned quickly that Mr. Bing wasn't much of a joker.)

So I stood there with the telephone in one hand and a mop in the other, wondering if this could possibly be Julie Baker playing a phone prank. I was about to say, "All right, Julie—can it," but I decided not to risk making the same mistake as Bert Lahr.

"Yes, Mr. Bing. What can I do for you?"

"My dear Miss Farrell, I have read time and again that the reason you have not appeared at the Metropolitan Opera is that you have never been asked. Well, I'm asking you now. Would you like to make your debut with us next season?"

"In which opera?"

"Gluck's *Alceste*. A new production."

Bing went on to explain that *Alceste* hadn't been done at the Met since Kirsten Flagstad had sung it as her company farewell in

1952. The fact that the Met was willing to mount a new production for me meant that they were taking me seriously. I didn't know the whole opera, but I had sung Alceste's big aria, "Divinités du Styx," many times on my radio show.

"Will we do it in French?" I asked Mr. Bing.

"Oh, no," said Mr. Bing. "I don't have any French singers. We'll do it in an English translation."

I talked the offer over with Bob, and with Ruth O'Neill and Arthur Judson, and pretty soon it was official: I would make my debut at the Metropolitan Opera on December 6, 1960.

Some time earlier I had gotten to know Leontyne Price. How Leontyne ever achieved the success she did is a real tribute to her, because in spite of her phenomenal talent she had every strike in the book against her. There weren't many black singers—period—in her day, and it was unthinkable that one would become an opera star of Leontyne's magnitude. Sometime after I had received Bing's formal invitation, we both found ourselves at the San Francisco Opera. I was singing *Ariadne auf Naxos,* and she was doing Leonora in *Il trovatore.* Since I had done *Trovatore* in San Francisco not long before that, Leontyne asked me to come to her dress rehearsal and see what I thought. The conductor rushed like crazy through the first act, and poor Leontyne, struggling to keep up, started to push. I went backstage at the end of the first act and found her in tears. "I don't know how I'm going to get through this," she cried. "I can't sing it that fast!"

After I calmed her down as best as I could, we agreed to meet for dinner that night. We split a bottle of wine, which put Leontyne in a secret-sharing mood, and after her second glass, she leaned across the table and said, "I can't stand it anymore. I have to tell you, and you have to promise me not to tell anybody." She took another sip of wine, and her face broke into a big smile. "Next year, I'm going to be at the Met in *Il trovatore.*"

I said, "Well, Leontyne, I have something to tell you, and I want you to promise not to tell anybody. *I'm* going to be there, too."

She let out a whoop, and we drank to each other's success.

In addition to giving me a new production of *Alceste,* Rudolf Bing wanted me to sing some performances of Ponchielli's *La gioconda* a few weeks after *Alceste* opened. During 1960, I worked hard with Miss Mac getting both operas in shape. I was sorry that Bing had decided not to do *Alceste* in French. The minute I took a look at the Met's English translation by John Gutman, I thought we were done for. It was just awful, and in rehearsal we changed a lot of the words that were too awkward to pronounce. I was already starting to get the idea that Rudolf Bing had his own peculiar way of doing things. He'd told me that we wouldn't be doing *Alceste* in French because he didn't have any French singers, then turned around and cast Nicolai Gedda, a master of French style, as Admète. I knew I'd be in good hands with the conductor, Erich Leinsdorf, because we had worked well together in a number of Wagner concerts from the midfifties on. The production was directed and designed by Michael Manuel, and Anthony Tudor was the choreographer.

Ruth O'Neill was thrilled that I was making my Met debut and was sure that I was going to have a great career there. Edgar Vincent worked overtime during the fall of 1960 generating publicity. Today, it's hard to believe that the mainstream press would pay so much attention to a Met debut, but the newspapers and magazines were all over the story: There seemed to be a feeling that I was kind of an underdog, a valued American singer who had been snubbed by the Met for too long. The fact that I *was* American was actually part of the problem. When Rudolf Bing came to the Met in 1950, he didn't bend over backward to engage American artists. His interest was mainly in European singers who had been prevented from coming over to the United

States during the war. Eleanor Steber had an especially hard time there. She could sing a huge repertory beautifully, but Bing never gave her the respect she deserved.

Even though Bing could have invited me to sing before he did, the timing of my Met debut wasn't bad. At this point, I was mostly interested in singing the Italian repertory. *La gioconda* was a role I especially liked, and if I was going to expand my opera repertoire, I wanted it to be centered around Italian roles. I kept getting pushed to do Wagner roles onstage, but I wasn't interested. Doing Wagner excerpts in concert was as far down that road as I wanted to go; building a career around Wagner had killed off many sopranos. At the time, I had the idea that my voice was a little too schmaltzy for Wagner; it always seemed to me better suited to Italian roles, although plenty of people disagreed with me. Besides, Birgit Nilsson had come along and made such a splash with her Met debut in 1959 that I was happy to leave Wagner territory to her.

From the start, I didn't like Rudolf Bing at all. He was a snob, and he was determined to show he was the boss. He also had a nasty, sarcastic edge that was hard to take. I wasn't wild about some of his associates, either. His main gofer was Bob Herman, who had a terrific sense of his own importance but was weak when it came to musical background. (Erich Leinsdorf, among others, felt the Bing administration was damaged over the years because Herman was in over his head in too many areas.) The press officer, Francis Robinson, wasn't a favorite of mine, either. He wasn't affected, exactly, but he wasn't genuine and down-to-earth either. There was something slippery about him, and he was every inch the company man. I didn't feel comfortable around any of these people, but I told myself that wasn't important. I just tried to concentrate on my job and make sure my debut would be a success.

That fall, I reported to the Met for rehearsals. I may not have hit it off with the Met's top brass, but I got on very well with the stage crew. I got so friendly with them that when they were going to be given an award by their union, they asked me to accept it on their behalf. I'll never forget how they came to my rescue during rehearsals of *Alceste*. The day we moved onto the main stage to rehearse, I had a terrible allergic reaction to something. I'd never had a sinus problem in my life, but all of a sudden, I was miserable. When I left the Met at the end of the day, I felt better immediately, so it was obviously something on the stage. I went to the doctor, and he told me to bring him some sweepings from the stage floor. I asked the stage crew if they could help me, and they presented me with a big shoebox full of sweepings, all tied up with a big kelly green ribbon. There were a lot of dances in *Alceste,* and it turned out that I was allergic to the rosin on the dancer's shoes. My doctor came up with a vaccine, and from then on I was fine. As for *Alceste* itself, I was never all that crazy about it. There wasn't much that was wonderful to sing apart from "Divinités du Styx."

Usually I tried not to let my singing interfere with life at home any more than it had to, but since my Met debut was such a big deal, I decided to move into Manhattan for the final week of rehearsals so I wouldn't have to keep going back and forth to Staten Island. I checked into a suite at the Plaza and left Bob to handle things at home.

I wasn't too prone to stage fright until much later in my career, but my debut at the Met was a nerve-wracking one, and the company didn't do anything to make it easier for me. Even after all my years on radio and the hoopla over *Medea,* Bing had underestimated my New York following and scheduled *Alceste*'s opening night as a regular subscription performance. A huge block of tickets was already out to subscribers before single tickets became available, and the demand for singles was way ahead of the supply. A couple of weeks or so before my debut, Bob got a call from Dick

Daley, a judge on Staten Island who was a good friend of ours. He said he had called the Met box office to order tickets and was told that nothing was available "because a certain lady from Staten Island had bought out the house." I was upset, and Bob went right through the ceiling. If the Met was really telling this to the public, it would look as if I was nervous about my success and wanted to make sure I had a cheering section in place.

Bob called Ruth O'Neill and Edgar Vincent and asked them to get to the bottom of it. Edgar called Francis Robinson, who questioned the Met box-office staff and said that no one would admit to saying such a thing. Francis behaved in true company-man style. He just couldn't believe it had happened, and he told Bob that Dick Daley must have misunderstood. Bob was furious. When he got angry, his face got very red and his voice, very high, and he sounded more like a police-glee-club tenor than ever. He got on the phone and screamed at Francis, "I would rather have my wife chained to the radiator than sing at the Met on Tuesday night." He had just gotten calmed down when he got a call from Bill Fisher of the Gramma Fisher Foundation, which gave a lot of money to the Met. Bill Fisher was giving a party for me at the St. Regis after the performance on opening night. We had been asked for a guest list, and we submitted a small one—my mother, my brother, John, and his family, Aunt Helen, and a couple of friends—it couldn't have been more than twelve people. Now, after the box-office mess, Mr. Fisher said to Bob, "The list for your opening-night party is getting a little long. I wonder, would you mind taking a few people off it?"

Bob's voice went up again.

"I'll tell you what we'll do, Mr. Fisher," he said. "You pay for half of the party, and I'll pay for the other half."

"Oh, that's fine, Mr. Reagan. Thank you so much."

That was our welcome to the Met. I was starting to think I'd have been better off back on *The Garry Moore Show.*

My Met debut, with Nicolai Gedda
in Gluck's *Alceste,* December 6, 1960.
The opera had been absent from
the Met's repertory since Kirsten
Flagstad's farewell, and it hasn't been
back since the year Nicolai and I did
it. Photograph by Peter Stackpole,
Life Magazine, copyright Time Inc.

December 6 finally came. *Life* magazine had a photographer in the wings to cover the event. Mother and Aunt Helen, and John, Sylvia, and their kids were all staying in Manhattan. Robbie had flown down from his prep school in Massachusetts, and we'd gotten him a tux. We'd bought Kathy a special outfit, too—a little black-and-white dress, a black velvet pocketbook, and white kid gloves. Everyone was very excited. I was too frantic to pay much attention to what was going on.

While I was resting in my hotel that day, I got a phone call from Kathleen.

"Mommy?" Her voice sounded weak and hoarse. My heart sank.

"What's wrong, baby?" I asked.

"I've got the measles."

"Oh, honey. Oh, my God. Has anyone called the doctor? What's your temperature? Put your father on the phone."

Long silence. Then:

"What's the matter, Mommy? Have you lost your sense of humor?"

After remonstrating with Kathleen that it wasn't nice to try to kill her mother on the day of her Met debut, I glanced at the clock. It was time to leave for the Met. My heart pounded away while I showered, got dressed, and made my way down the hall to the elevator. Halfway down, the elevator stopped, and a young girl got on.

"Oh, Miss Farrell," she said, "I'm so glad I ran into you. Do you by any chance have an extra ticket to the Met tonight?"

"No, I'm sorry."

"But I called the Met, and they told me you had bought up the house."

My blood pressure shot up again. Maybe I was going to get off easy and have a stroke before I actually had to set foot onstage.

I was so nervous before my debut that I can hardly remember it. Only one thing stands out. Nicolai Gedda and I were standing up on one of the production's giant pedestals, and I was supposed to begin "Divinités du Styx" as I made my way down a long, steep staircase. When I began the aria, a dry-ice machine in the wings would start up to create a fog effect. It had all worked fine at the dress rehearsal, but on opening night, as I started to make my way down the steps, the steam from the dry ice floated up. The steps weren't even, so I had to hug the wall and make my way down very carefully—all the while singing "Divinités du Styx"! I was petrified, but I got through the aria. That was the moment everyone had been waiting for. There was a big wave of applause, and I can't remember a thing about the rest of the performance.

Suddenly, my debut was history. All the months of planning and work, and it's all over as quickly as Christmas morning. At the curtain calls, the production team took their lumps. Michael Manuel got booed, and so did the dancers. The audience hadn't liked what Tudor did at all, and the critics hated it—they felt it was too serious and not nearly theatrical enough. My housekeeper, Astrid Mortensen, had brought Kathleen down to the railing in front of the orchestra so she could see my curtain call up close. A couple of guys behind them started booing the dancers, and Kathleen, all decked out in her new dress and kid gloves, turned around and yelled, "IF YOU BOO MY MOMMY, I'LL SMACK YOU WITH MY PURSE!"

They didn't boo me. There was a huge ovation, and I kept getting called out onstage. I was later told that I got a grand total of twenty-two curtain calls.

It was time to enjoy myself. When I had arrived at the Met that evening, my dressing room table had been stacked with congratulatory telegrams, but I'd been too nervous to read them. Now I ripped them open.

"Sorry not able to attend your debut tonight. I am on a con-

A hug from Kathleen after my Met
debut in *Alceste*. Courtesy of the
Metropolitan Opera Archives.

cert tour in Canada. For many years I have known your beautiful voice and your rightful place in the sun. I wish you all the luck in the world. Welcome home. Risë Stevens."

"Go Gluck Go. Skitch Henderson."

"Here at last is the night we have all been waiting for. Hooray for you and Miss Mac. Peggy Wood."

Others were from Jimmie Fassett, Carol Fox, Roberta Peters, Regina Resnik, Claramae Turner, Mabel Mercer, George Trovillo, and Bill Graham. There was even one from Kukla, Fran, and Ollie! And a bottle of Champagne from Leontyne, who would make her debut a little over a month later, with a card that read, "To the President, from the Vice-President." After I read them, it was off to the St. Regis party—the one we helped pay for. It was a tremendous relief to have all the pressure taken off me, to have come through it in one piece. My personal notices for *Alceste* were very good, but since the critics clobbered the production, the Met never brought it back.

A couple of weeks later I sang *La gioconda,* which I liked singing much more than I did *Alceste.* At the time, Zinka Milanov was the Met's champion Gioconda, and when she sang the arietta just before Gioconda kills herself, she did a little stage business of tearing petals off some flowers. I refused to do anything so inane, and Edgar Vincent came up with the idea of singing the arietta directly into a mirror, which worked beautifully. Gioconda's story is a little weird—I mean, she spends the whole damned opera looking for her mother. At the end, she's still wandering around, calling, "Mom . . . Mom?" But the music is great. Part of the reason I've always loved *Gioconda* is that everybody—not just the soprano and tenor—gets a chance to shine with a big aria. I had wonderful mezzos as Laura—Regina Resnik and Nell Rankin. They were terrific colleagues, and I loved working with them. Then there was Richard Tucker.

Richard had one of the most gorgeous tenor voices I ever heard in my life. Unfortunately, he also had an unbelievable ego. His wife, Sara, was Jan Peerce's sister. Jan and I had been close friends for years, ever since we began singing in the Bach Aria Group together. Jan and Richard didn't have anything in common except Sara and their beautiful voices. Jan was modest, generous, thoughtful, fun-loving, and very concerned about the whole performance, not just his part of it. All Richard cared about was how Richard came off. I'm not sure he realized anyone else was on the stage with him. Everyone knew how much Richard and Jan disliked each other. Richard treated Jan terribly; he liked to tell people that the trouble between them came about because Jan couldn't stand being second-best. Well, I'm glad *he* thought so. Richard may have had a gorgeous voice, but having sung with both of them, I wouldn't hesitate to say that Jan was by far the better musician.

In 1962, Richard and I recorded an album of Italian opera duets for Columbia. Richard was terrified of doing anything—even recording—without his toupee. He held up the sessions at Manhattan Center because there was no dressing room for changing, just a men's room. Once his rug was in place, I thought we would just sail through it, but there was more trouble ahead. What can I say about my voice? It was LOUD, and while it was never a problem on my solo records, because the engineers knew just what to do, it was a problem when I was recording duets. Richard had a hefty voice himself, but I guess mine just carried more easily. The engineers kept asking me to back away from the microphone. I kept backing up and backing up until I was practically at Newark Airport. The problems didn't end when we finished the recording.

The official name of the album was *Great Duets from Verdi Operas with Eileen Farrell and Richard Tucker*. Richard went through the roof when he found out it had been released that way, and he ordered Columbia to switch the billing on the second print run. My managers found out about it, and Columbia restored the original billing, but not before many copies had hit the record stores with Richard's name ahead of mine. There are probably some diehard LP collectors out there who have both versions.

At the Met, I also worked with Franco Corelli. After my successful debut, Bing invited me to open the 1962–63 season in Giordano's *Andrea Chénier*. I was thrilled, because the role of Maddalena, the aristocrat whose life is turned upside down by the French Revolution, was something I could really sink my teeth into. Corelli starred opposite me as the poet Chénier. Bob Merrill was Gérard, the embittered servant who becomes a revolutionary leader. It was an honor to be chosen to open the Met season, especially after I'd been there such a short time. The performances of *Chénier* were pretty wild, though. Corelli was at the peak of his form, but he had the worst stage fright I'd ever seen. He would show up for rehearsal and sing beautifully, then all of a sudden he'd throw up his hands and say that he was in terrible voice and couldn't go on. Singing seemed to be agony for him, and once the run began, I started to see why he was such a wreck. At intermission, his wife Loretta would barricade herself in his dressing room and scream at him, telling him everything he'd done wrong. She didn't shut up even when we were onstage. I got so I would try to avoid going to extreme stage left or right, no matter what the blocking called for, because Signora Corelli was always in the wings, yelling at her husband in Italian, and I'd have to concentrate like crazy to stay on track.

I'd done only a few operas, but already I was getting the feeling that maybe this wasn't for me. In radio, in television, even, for the most part, in the concert world, I had been used to everyone pulling together and trying to get the show in shape. We all worked hard but had fun in the process. Opera was something

With Richard Tucker. We weren't
nearly as chummy as we look in this
photo. Courtesy of Photofest.

Franco Corelli and I opened the
Met's 1962–63 season in *Andrea
Chénier.* This picture gives a good
indication of how much I liked
working with Corelli. Photograph
by Louis Mélançon, courtesy of
Opera News.

With Bob Merrill in *Andrea Chénier*.
I loved singing the part of
Maddalena, the aristocratic girl
caught up in the French Revolution.
Photograph copyright 1999 by
Paul Seligman.

else. There seemed to be very little sense of everyone working together toward a common goal; instead, I saw a lot of people who were interested only in how they came off and didn't give a damn about anything else.

Don't get me wrong—there were many wonderful colleagues at the Met. One of my favorites was Robert Merrill. Like me, Bob's background was show business. He had sung at the Roxy and Radio City Music Hall, been on radio, played the Borscht Belt circuit, and made a Hollywood movie, *Aaron Slick from Punkin Crick* (1951), so we always had a lot we could talk about together.

In 1961, we were cast in *La forza del destino* at the Met. I was the maiden, Leonora, who runs away with her lover, Don Alvaro (Richard Tucker again), after he accidentally kills her father. Don Alvaro is pursued for years by Leonora's brother, Don Carlo, played by Bob. At the end, Don Carlo lies dying, and the guilt-ridden Leonora stands over him. Bob was lying on the ground, and I was leaning over him, about a half-mile away from the orchestra, listening for my cue. I was craning my neck to hear, and all of a sudden Bob said, "Would you mind taking your left tit out of my mouth?" I started to laugh so hard I barely made the cue. I sat there, rocking back and forth with my shoulders shaking, thinking, "You sonofabitch. I'm going to get back at you."

Several days later we did *Forza* again. As usual, I was dieting, and in my dressing room I had a stash of Metrecal cookies. When I went onstage for that same scene, I took one of the cookies with me. I held it in my hand all during the aria, hoping it wouldn't melt under the hot lights, because I had plans for it. I walked over to where Bob was lying, whispered, "Here's a cookie to go with the milk," and slapped it on his chest.

At the Met, I also sang Santuzza in Mascagni's *Cavalleria rusticana*. Santuzza is unhappily in love with Turiddu, who has recently thrown her over for Lola, the town slut. Early in the opera, Santuzza sings the aria "Voi lo sapete," pouring out her problems to Turiddu's mother, Mamma Lucia. For several performances, Mamma Lucia was played by the great contralto Lili Chookasian. It was hard to get through "Voi lo sapete" with Lili, because as I tried to work myself up into a big emotional state, she would sit across the table from me and whisper, "No kidding?"

I would have made a lousy diva, and I never even tried to pull it off, but there were some women around the Met who were very good at it. Eleanor Steber was the champ. I always liked Eleanor. We had both been with Columbia Community Concerts, so I'd seen her quite a bit then, and I had seen her at the Met as Sophie in *Der Rosenkavalier*—God, she was marvelous. She was still at the Met when I got there, and she always had her entourage. She carried all that off like a one-egg cake before breakfast. Eleanor was quite the party girl, too. I remember one time when she had an early rehearsal at the Met, around nine in the morning. Eleanor came with a thermos bottle and a stack of paper cups. She offered to share it with one of her colleagues, who assumed it was coffee until she took a sip of it and found out it was Champagne. Well—good for Eleanor, I say.

It didn't take me long to figure out that I wasn't one of Bing's favorites. We started out being wary of one another, and we worked our way up to intense dislike. While I was in rehearsals for *Andrea Chénier,* there was a now-famous incident that made Bing furious. Earlier in the week, there had been a benefit for the Milk Fund in which a lot of the Met stars had sung. Bob Merrill was scheduled to perform, but something had come up and he'd had to cancel. The next day a review appeared in one of the New York newspapers praising Bob's performance. Bing was livid, and as I was rehearsing *Andrea Chénier,* he stormed onto the stage carrying a copy of the newspaper. It was standard for invited guests to be admitted to the final dress, but with our dress rehearsal of *Chénier* coming up, Bing told us that he was afraid someone from the press would turn up and write a review before we opened. The review might print more incorrect information, causing more embarrassment for the Met.

"There will be *nobody* allowed at dress rehearsal," Bing hissed. "No one can bring any guests in." His eyes moved from one company member to the next, and he finally decided to single me out for some special treatment.

"Farrell," he snapped, "That goes for Edgar Vincent and your husband, too."

"Fine," I said, "I'll tell my husband. He isn't interested, anyway." He gave me one more long, cold stare and stormed off the stage.

Bing could be funny at someone else's expense (usually a singer's), but he had no sense of humor about himself whatsoever. I found this out in a big way once when I was appearing in *Forza* on the Met's annual spring tour. Most everybody in the touring company traveled together on a train, carousing and playing cards all the way from Minneapolis to Cleveland to Dallas. Lots of them loved life on the road, but I thought traveling in close quarters with all those people—they used to call themselves "the Met family"—didn't sound like my idea of fun. Instead, I flew to meet them wherever they were performing. On the *Forza* tour, I got to Cleveland and found I was booked into the same hotel Bob Merrill was staying in and that Bing had a suite on the top floor. That night there was another opera on, one that Bob and I weren't in. Over dinner, Bob mentioned that after the performance there was going to be a party in Bing's suite.

"Of course, even though we're not singing tonight, we'll have to go to the party," he said.

"Forget it," I said. "I'm not going to stay up half the night at some stupid party. If you want me, I'll be in my room with my feet up."

Bob had had his own problems with Bing. In the early 1950s he'd temporarily kissed the Met good-bye for a fling in the movies, which hadn't panned out very well. He'd had to swallow his pride, admit he'd been a bust in Hollywood, and come crawling back to the Met. Bing eventually welcomed him back into the fold, but he always reminded Bob who was boss after that, and Bob didn't want to rock the boat again.

"Oh, come on, Eileen," said Bob. "We'll be expected to go. I'm going, and you're going with me."

I finally gave in, and Bob and I turned up at Bing's suite at the appointed hour. We walked in, and I could hardly believe what I saw: Everyone in the company was sitting there, as polite as could be, hands folded, just like in school. No one was talking much, and absolutely nobody was laughing.

"I thought you said this was a party," I said to Bob.

Some of the Met's biggest stars were sitting there acting like good little boys and girls, afraid to step out of line in case they'd get detention.

I went over to where Leontyne Price was sitting. She was smiling a very broad, tense, smile.

"Boy, does this look like a lot of fun," I said.

"I don't know what you mean," said Leontyne, her smile getting even bigger.

After a while, someone put on a record of pop music, and Leontyne got up the nerve to dance with somebody. Things seemed to be loosening up a little, so I went over to Bing, who was sitting on a sofa.

"May I have this dance?" I asked.

There was a long, stony silence. Then he said, "I *don't* dance."

"Well," I said, "how are you ever going to get to be successful if you don't dance?"

Bing didn't think this was funny at all. He just sat there, staring at me. Just then I felt Bob Merrill's hand on my arm.

"We have to leave," said Bob. "Thanks very much, Mr. Bing.
Lovely party."

Bob hustled me out in the hallway.

"What in the hell is the matter with you?" he snapped, his
hands shaking. "I could have killed you! Don't *ever* do anything
like that again!"

That was the Met family.

Lots of opera singers have special routines they follow on performance days. The most careful ones refuse to speak one word
all day unless they have to, and a lot of others speak only a little.
Some of them need extensive warm-ups before the performance,
others warm up just a little, and most of them are very fussy about
what they eat beforehand—a little breast of chicken, some clear
soup, or maybe a green salad.

When I sang at the Met, I had a routine, too. With Robbie
and Kathy running around raising hell, it was pointless to think
about not speaking. Kids are sensitive, and I thought if I played
the grand diva and refused to talk to them, it would hurt them
too much. I tried not to yell unless necessary; otherwise, I carried on pretty much normally. At some point around midday, I
would go into the music room and sing through the entire opera.
Some people think this is crazy, but I say if you're going to be
singing high Cs that night, you'd better make sure they're in
place that afternoon.

Late in the afternoon I would take the Staten Island ferry,
and once I got to Manhattan, I would jump in a taxi and head
for the Met. There was a little restaurant just across the street
where I would always go for a six-o'clock dinner. I usually had

the same thing—a steak, baked potato, green salad, and hot tea with lemon. Rich, creamy desserts really clog up your throat, so I would order a dish of Jell-O, which went down very easily. Then I'd go across the street, hit my dressing room, and get into my makeup and costume. The only thing I insisted on having in my dressing room when I arrived was a big bottle of warm Coca-Cola. Once I was in my costume, I would drink a few glasses of warm Coke and start to belch. It's amazing what this can do for the voice, and as Miss Mac always used to tell me, "It saves wear and tear on the rectum." I remember that Beverly Sills was scandalized when we were singing together at Lewisohn Stadium in the early '50s, and she heard me ripping off one after another in my dressing room. "Those weren't discreet burps," Beverly told me recently. "They were more like symphonies."

I had a routine for after the performance, too. Bob would usually pick me up at the Met, and after I had greeted the backstage visitors and autographed programs, we would pile into the car and drive back to Staten Island. On the New Jersey Turnpike, there was a Howard Johnson's where we would always go, and I would order a frankfurter and a tall glass of cold milk. No matter what the opera was, I would look forward all night to my 1 A.M. snack at Howard Johnson's.

All in all, I spent five seasons at the Met: 1960–61 through 1963–64, and again in 1965–66. *Alceste* was the only new production I ever got, but I was perfectly happy singing in revivals of the meat-and-potatoes Italian operas. Vocally, I felt most comfortable there, and I started to get very nervous whenever anyone started talking about complete Wagner roles. Lots of my colleagues thought it would be to my advantage, as well as the Met's, if I moved in that direction, but I stood my ground. I'd heard stories about singers with wonderful voices who'd wrecked themselves the minute they tried to cross over into Wagner. The great American baritone Leonard Warren sang Verdi magnificently, but earlier in his career, the Met had tried to turn him into a Wagnerian, and he'd practically had a breakdown trying to make the switch. I wanted none of it, and when Bing offered me Ortrud in *Lohengrin,* I turned him down flat.

This didn't make him very happy, but he had bigger problems to worry about. The old Met was going to be torn down, and the company was moving into its new home at Lincoln Center beginning with the 1966–67 season. About a year before the move, my husband and I were summoned to Bing's office to discuss repertory for the first season at the new house.

Resting on the edge of Bing's desk was a giant riding crop. It was so strange that you couldn't just ignore it, so I decided to try to make a joke out of it.

"Is that what you use on tenors?" I asked.

"Oh, no, no," he said, as he picked up the riding crop. He twisted it in the middle and pulled it apart. Inside was a gleaming stiletto. Bob and I were speechless as Bing pointed the stiletto toward me and gave me a tight little smile.

"My dear Miss Farrell," he said, "I would very much like you to sing Marie in *Wozzeck* next season. In English."

"Well, I'm sorry," I said. "I did it in German at Carnegie Hall, and I'll be happy to do it here, but it's just too much work to relearn it in English."

He stared at me with those piercing eyes. After one of his deadly pauses, he said, "Perhaps I should leave the two of you alone to discuss this."

Ever since *Alceste,* the stagehands had warned me that Bing had microphones in his office. I don't know if this was true or not, but they swore the mikes were connected to the stage, so that he could flip a switch in his office and hear what was being said at rehearsal. If a singer was saying things about him behind his back, Bing could monitor the situation and dole out punishment.

Bing left the room, closing the door behind him. I'd heard this was a favorite trick of his, too. During negotiations, he would leave the room and the singer and his agent or spouse would discuss whatever offer had just been made. Usually they'd have a few pointed words about Bing and the Met, and sometimes they would find out that everything they said had been recorded. Bob put his fingers to his lips, and we sat there making idle conversation.

"What are we having for dinner tonight?" asked Bob in a stage voice.

"Pork roast," I said. "Remind me to pick up some onions at the supermarket on the way home."

This went on for a little longer until Bing came back into the office.

"Have you reached a final decision?" he asked.

"Yes," said Bob. "We're sorry, but we still have to say no to *Wozzeck* in English."

"I see," said Bing. "Well, thank you for coming in."

That was it. We were escorted out, and as we stepped out onto Broadway, it suddenly hit me that these performances of *Andrea Chénier* would be my last at the Met. I had turned down both Ortrud and Marie, and you didn't say no to Rudolf Bing twice.

I was right. Herbert Barrett, who had replaced Ruth O'Neill as my agent, called Bing's office toward the end of the 1965–66 season to see what the Met had lined up for me the following year.

"I'm sorry," said Bing. "Please tell Miss Farrell we have nothing for her." Then he added a real Bing-style twist of the knife: "Of course, if she likes, I could ask one of our foreign artists to relinquish one performance for her."

Barrett relayed the message back to me and this time I was the one who hit the ceiling.

"Tell him no, thank you," I said. In those days, the Met often left your name on the artist roster even if you weren't singing. "And you can also tell him," I said, "to take my name off the roster."

I reported to the Met that spring for *Andrea Chénier*. At the end of the opera, Maddalena and Chénier climb the stairs to the scaffold to be executed. Earlier that season, Renata Tebaldi had sung Maddalena, and because she had trouble with the stairs, the ending had been restaged and the stairs taken out to make it easier for her. Franco Corelli was my Chénier again, and when we had done it in 1962–63, we used the original staging, with the staircase. Now Corelli decided he didn't want to come to rehearsal. "I already did it with Farrell a couple of years ago," he told Bing, who, of course, let him get away with it. Opening night came around, and once again I didn't have any idea what he might do onstage. To make matters worse, during the reunion scene, Corelli grabbed me and kissed me right on the mouth— something that had never happened before. A lot of women would have given anything to be put in that position, but it threw me off so badly I wanted to kill him.

That was it—the end of five seasons at the Met. It was a thrill to be part of that tradition, even for a short time.

It's always seemed strange to me that the most important opera house in the world allowed itself to be controlled by so much arrogance and pettiness. Bing ruled by intimidation, and back then, at least, the Met was a real house of fear. I've never been able to understand why the company seemed so hell-bent on making life difficult for so many people. They didn't seem to understand then (I don't know what it's like today) that singers have a much better chance of giving their best performance if they're treated well, and if the whole working process is a happy

With Corelli and Bob Merrill, one
of my all-time favorite colleagues, in
Andrea Chénier. Courtesy of the
Metropolitan Opera Archives.

one. Many great singers have never appeared there at all, and many others were cast in the wrong roles or in cheap productions with inadequate rehearsal, making it impossible for them to do their best work. Callas may have been the greatest singing artist of the 1950s, but she couldn't conquer the Met. Looking back, I see that I was never at ease there from the first day I set foot in the place, and it was probably unavoidable that I wouldn't stick around too long.

In the 1970s, when Schuyler Chapin took over as general manager, he wrote to me several times asking me to come back. By then I was teaching full-time at Indiana University, and a run of Met performances would have been impossible to schedule. And really, I had no desire to return. When I first came to the Met, I wasn't a newcomer eager to please; I had twenty years of professional singing behind me, and I was set in my ways. So it was probably harder for me to fit in than it would have been for a lot of people. But now that I no longer sing, the one thing I miss is standing on the Met stage behind the great gold curtain, watching the dust fly up through a shaft of light, hearing the orchestra play the introduction to the last act of *Forza* or *Gioconda* or *Chénier,* feeling that something wonderful was about to happen.

CHAPTER TEN

Y NAME is Bob," my husband used to say when he introduced himself to people—"That's Bob. With one *o*." Bob loved to joke around with people he liked, but if he thought you didn't belong, you knew it soon enough. He was a tough guy, and he didn't waste time on anybody who didn't meet his standards. If he sensed somebody was trying to take advantage of me, personally or professionally, that person was out in the cold. Bob's childhood had done a lot to make him as hard-nosed as he was. He was an only child and very strong-willed, and his parents found him hard to handle. I still have a letter his mother wrote to him when he had gone away to visit relatives: "Dear Robert: Received your card. Glad you are having a wonderful time down in Delaware. Please try and take good care of yourself because things happen to boys who don't, so take your mother's advice just for once in a lifetime. Go to church and pray that you will amount to something someday. Keep well with God's help. Your mother."

Bob's father had a different way of keeping him in line; he

used to beat the living daylights out of him on a fairly regular basis. When Bob was twelve, his mother died, and his father remarried. Bob's stepmother didn't want much to do with him, and before long Bob went to live with two old-maid aunts who spoiled him terribly. He went to St. Peter's High School on Staten Island, and after he graduated he became a union bus driver, also on Staten Island. A few years later, he enrolled in the police academy and eventually joined the NYPD, where he served for twenty years. Because Bob and his first wife got an annulment in the state, which the Catholic Church wouldn't recognize, Bob and I were excommunicated for the first twenty years of our marriage. Even though we couldn't receive sacrament, we went to Mass regularly, and our kids were baptized in the faith and attended Catholic school—Robbie until his junior year in college, and Kathleen until her sophomore year in high school.

Bob was ten and a half years older than I was; he was pushing forty when Robbie was born. He'd waited a long time to have children, and being a father was probably the greatest thrill of his life—he was never too busy to spend time with his kids. I hardly ever saw him so much as swat Robbie and Kathleen. After the way his own father had treated him, it was next to impossible for him to lay hands on his own kids. I've known fathers who refused to change their children's diapers, but that wasn't Bob's way at all.

Bob really didn't like New York at all, even though he'd lived there all his life. Eventually we started spending a good chunk of each year up in Maine, and I think it was probably the most important move we ever made as a family. It all started purely by accident.

For years, I suffered from terrible gall bladder attacks. Once, when George Trovillo and I were in Cincinnati for the May Festival, I had an attack while we were in a taxi on our way to the performance. By the time we got to the Music Hall, I was in terrible pain and could barely catch my breath. "You have to get a doctor to give me a shot of morphine," I told George, and he asked the management to find someone, fast.

Pretty soon a doctor showed up, looking like he wandered in off the set of *Gunsmoke*. He wore a bolo tie and cowboy boots and carried a little black bag. When he walked into my dressing room, he said, "You need to lose weight!"

"Thanks!" I said. "But I'm having a gall bladder attack."

"How do you know?"

"Because I'm about to die! Give me the goddam morphine!"

He gave me a shot and the pain vanished almost immediately. The concert went off without a hitch, but when I came offstage at the end, I said to George, "That's the last attack I'm ever going to have." When I got back to the East Coast, I went straight up to Boston to the Lahey Clinic and had my surgery. It went fine, but I had a tube stuck in me, and my doctor warned me, "Absolutely no singing for the rest of the summer." Bob and I decided that as long as I couldn't work, we might as well take the kids and go away for a while.

First we tried Kezar Lake in New Hampshire. Bob found a lovely little rental cottage that had one drawback: There was no shower. You had to bathe in the lake, and when you broke out the soap, all the leeches suddenly came out. They were so bad that I had to keep a pair of tweezers down by the lake all the time. After a couple of summers there, Bob said, "I think I'll look around some more." We went up to Moosehead Lake in west-central Maine, and we loved the setting. We rented a house there for a couple of summers, and then Bob found a fabulous two-story house surrounded by pine trees, with a boathouse and a seventy-two-foot dock, nestled in a beautiful little cove. It was perfect. We fixed it up and it became our summer getaway for the next twenty-five years.

Every June, at the end of my concert season, we would pack up our station wagon, hitch our boat onto the back, and head up to Moosehead Lake. In the station wagon we had the four of us; Astrid Mortensen, our housekeeper; and our two dogs. The boat was loaded up with suitcases and a television set and everything else we could think of to get us through the summer. This was long before there was Interstate 95 or any of the other freeways that shoot up north today, and it was a long, beautiful, peaceful drive.

Our life in Maine was so different from the one we led in New York that Bob always said it saved us both from heart attacks. There were wild berries growing everywhere, and beautiful lilies right next to the shore. Back then, the salmon fishing was marvelous. (That was before Scott Paper Company, which owned a lot of the land in northern Maine, drained the lake so the logs could come through; a lot of the salmon died because they lay their eggs close to shore, and there wasn't enough water to cover them.) Every evening after dinner, Bob and I would go out in the boat and fish until it got dark. This was our time alone together. Often we could see the Milky Way, and the aroma of pine was even stronger at night.

I found I could get a tremendous amount of practicing done in such a peaceful setting. I had a Baldwin studio piano shipped up so I could work on learning new music over the summer. One year George Trovillo came up, and we worked on *Ariadne auf Naxos*.

I loved Maine. I couldn't wait to get there in the summer— but when fall came around, I was definitely ready to get back to New York and start singing again.

In the midfifties, with my career swinging away, Bob took a full retirement after twenty years with the NYPD. He'd covered a lot of ground on the force; in his early days, he'd pounded a beat in

Chinatown, and by the time I met him, he was on the forgery squad at Center Street. Later on, he worked out of the district attorney's office on Staten Island, and when he retired, he was working in children's safety. His schedule had always varied. One week it would be 8 A.M. to 4 P.M., the next week 4 to midnight, and he couldn't wait to hang it up so he could spend more time with the kids. He loved to read and buried himself every day in the newspapers (never *The New York Times*). He also read the *National Review* cover to cover, and every political biography he could get his hands on.

Even though Bob was retired, he couldn't give up his gun. He still wore it, even around the house. Like a lot of retired cops, he claimed his hip got cold without it. I'm sure a lot of my musician friends thought it was a little strange, but around the Reagan house, Daddy always packed a heater.

As much as Bob loved music, he really wasn't a musician, and he never tried to advise me on what I should and shouldn't sing. But now that he was no longer working, he started paying closer attention to my career. He had a keen business sense, and I remember him saying one day, "You know, all this work you're doing isn't going to be worth much if all you have to show for it at the end is a bunch of canceled checks." So Bob invested our money, kept it where it was, and did very well with it. (Bob's Uncle Vincie worked on Wall Street, and he told Bob not to buy and sell every time he turned around.) Thanks to Bob, I still get five checks a month from those investments.

Probably the roughest spots in our marriage were caused by Bob's possessiveness. From the beginning, he felt insecure around my music friends because they shared a part of me that he couldn't. He'd always been jealous of anyone who took up my time, personally or professionally, but after he retired, it became much worse. I would make friends with someone, and immediately Bob would try to persuade me that whoever it was had an

The Reagans at home. Notice that
Daddy's packing his heater. Courtesy
of United Press International.

ulterior motive. Working on the police force for all those years had helped him develop a suspicious mind. He didn't trust Tommy Schippers at all, and he was especially jealous of the time I spent on tour with the Bach Aria Group. Now and then I would invite Julie Baker, Bernie Greenhouse, and some of the other members of the group over for dinner, and I would spend the entire evening tied in knots, wondering if Bob was going to say something to embarrass me in front of the gang.

Being half Italian and half Irish, Bob got a charge out of rubbing people the wrong way. After he retired, he always said it was his job "to manage the managers." I don't think he ever trusted anyone who represented me after Horace Parmelee. Bob figured that if anything should happen to Uncle Horace, all the slimy managers in New York would be circling over me, so he had it put in my contract with Columbia that if Uncle Horace died, Bill Judd and Ruth O'Neill of the firm Judson, O'Neill and Judd would automatically become my managers. Some time in the midfifties Uncle Horace passed away, and off I went to Judson, O'Neill and Judd. Old Arthur Judson wasn't too involved in my career; all he really did was occasionally suggest that I do one piece or another. Once he called to ask me if I knew Strauss's Four Last Songs. I said no, and he said, "Well, I suggest you learn them, because the Cincinnati Symphony is coming to New York, and I think you should do it with them." So I learned them, but I hated singing them—four or five gorgeous bars, and all of a sudden the center of the piece slips out from under you, and you don't know *where* in the hell you are.

Mostly, my business was handled by Bill Judd and Ruth O'Neill. Bill was calm and quiet, and Ruth did most of the talking. She was an Irishwoman, and I'm afraid she'd done much more to the Blarney stone than just kiss it. Bob didn't trust Ruth from the get-go. The trouble started when I made my first trip to Europe in the summer of 1959. Both Bill Judd and Ruth

O'Neill came with me, and we had a marvelous trip over on the *Queen Mary*. After I got back, a check arrived from Columbia Artists with a whole list of deductions: I had paid for renting Albert Hall, for the orchestra, and for the boat tickets for everyone. No one had bothered to explain this to me—I assumed Albert Hall was a presentation, and if I'd known it was a rental, I wouldn't have bothered crossing the ocean.

Another time, I received my monthly statement from Judson, O'Neill and Judd, and there was one item that caught Bob's eye: We'd been charged over $200 for telegrams. Bob called Ruth's office and demanded a copy of every telegram they'd sent out under my name. When we got them in the mail, we saw that they were all messages to colleagues, saying things like, "Congratulations on your debut," and "Good luck at tonight's performance"—telegrams we'd never asked them to send. There were a few too many incidents like this for Bob Reagan's liking, and in the early '60s I left Judson, O'Neill and Judd and signed with Herbert Barrett, who handled me through the '70s.

Bob felt more at ease around the people in TV and show biz than the ones in classical music, and so did I. But the people who impressed him most were political figures. A staunch Republican, he was a big admirer of William F. Buckley, and had a long and friendly correspondence with him over the years. One night, Shirley Cowell's mother, Ione, gave a party for Dwight D. Eisenhower just before he was going to run for president. Eisenhower asked me to sing something, and then Ione asked Bob to sing. Bob turned his police glee club tenor loose on an Irish song, and Eisenhower was moved practically to tears.

We were invited to the White House several times—twice when Lyndon Johnson was president, and Bob was pleased, even if Johnson was a Democrat. But it was really a thrill in the 1980s, when President Reagan invited us for a special Saint Patrick's Day lunch. Bob idolized Reagan, and he was beside himself with

With President Eisenhower. I always
preferred posing with Republican
presidents. Personal collection of
Eileen Farrell.

excitement. It was quite a day: Maureen O'Hara was at our table, too. After lunch, an Irish tenor got up and sang "Danny Boy." I looked over and saw that President Reagan had tears in his eyes. He leaned over to me and whispered, "You know, I never really listened to the words before. That's the saddest song I ever heard."

During my early days of concertizing, Bob more than once kept me from flushing my whole career down the drain. I would get strung out by being away on tour for two weeks at a time, away from the kids, and I would come home in tears, screaming, "I'm never going to sing again! It's not worth it!" Then I'd call Horace Parmelee and tell him to cancel all my engagements and slam down the phone, and poor Uncle Horace would collapse at his desk. In a little while, Bob would call him back and say, "She doesn't mean it. It's all right—I'll talk to her."

One person Bob did not like was Goddard Lieberson, president of Columbia Records. Schuyler Chapin was Goddard's right-hand man. We all had a terrible blowup in the middle of the '60s, after my contract with Columbia expired. We had agreed to renew for another five years with a fixed guarantee of so much money. One Sunday afternoon, Schuyler and a couple of his sons came out to Staten Island for lunch. At some point during the afternoon, Schuyler said, "Oh, by the way, we've been talking it over, and there's a problem with that contract." He went on to explain that Columbia wouldn't be able to come across with the royalty arrangement we'd all agreed on—it would be a little bit lower.

Well, you just didn't say that to Bob Reagan. Everything had been settled; Bob thought Goddard's and Schuyler's handshakes should be as good as a written contract, and he was furious.

"Then forget the whole thing," Bob said.

Schuyler turned green. "Oh, no, no," he said. "We don't *want* to forget it."

"But *we* want to forget it," said Bob. When Schuyler left our house that day, it was the end of my association with Columbia Records—and for some reason, another major label never offered me a long-term contract.

To a certain extent, I needed Bob to look after my business. He was much smarter about managing money than I ever thought of being, and he didn't shy away from confrontation the way I did. I'd been that way since childhood—I would walk ten miles out of my way to avoid going head to head with *anybody*. So when Bob squared off against someone important in the music business or made an impulsive decision about my career, I kept my mouth shut. I have to admit that as time went on, it became harder and harder to say nothing.

Even without a recording contract, I was still awfully busy doing concerts throughout the '60s. I did some opera, too, although I still wasn't crazy about it and gradually phased it out of my schedule by about 1967. One that I missed out on was *Mourning Becomes Electra,* by my friend Marvin David Levy. I still have a letter he wrote to me, asking me if I'd be interested in playing the mother's part, Christine:

"Dear Eileen: The part of Christine made Nazimova famous in 1931. Though it is less famous than the part of Lavinia, it is much more intense and overwhelming and human. This is a synopsis. I don't have an extra libretto in hand. I'd be interested in your reaction. You sounded exquisite the other night and you're looking more beautiful every time I see you. Do hope to see you before you leave. I'll be here working on the opera until the end of the year. Love, Marvin."

I don't remember why I never wound up doing it, but it finally got to the Met in 1967, with Marie Collier as Christine and Evelyn Lear as Lavinia.

One of my best pals during this period was the comedian

Charles Nelson Reilly. Charles is not only a wonderful actor and director, he's also a big opera fan. He used to come to see me all the time at the Met on his nights off from *Hello, Dolly!* or *Sky-scraper* or whatever Broadway show he happened to be in at the time, and we became close friends. Later on, he went out to Hollywood to do the TV series *The Ghost and Mrs. Muir,* and whenever I was out in L.A. doing a concert or TV show, I would stay with Charles. Once when I was at his place, he put on one of the *Senza Voce* recordings. I was singing along with "Ritorna, vincitor!" while I washed the dishes. Just then, a delivery man came to the door and heard me.

"Your wife has a beautiful voice," he said to Charles. Then he turned to me and said, "You know, ma'am, you really should think about singing professionally."

"Oh, thank you," I said, "but I'd be too shy to sing in front of people."

Another time when I flew out to L.A., Charles met me at the airport with a silver bucket of Champagne. He told me that we were going to a nightclub to see the female impersonator Charles Pierce. "Dear Abby's going with us," he said.

That evening we drove over to Abigail Van Buren's house. Charles wasn't exactly sure where it was, but he said, "Just keep your eye out for the house that looks like it's been treated with hair spray." Sure enough, we found it. "Dear Abby" asked us to come in and have a drink before we went to the nightclub. She opened her refrigerator, and there was a whole shelf of little individual glasses of white wine. Very strange. We had a couple of drinks and went on to the show.

Charles Pierce was hilarious, as always. At the end of his act, he introduced the celebrities in the audience. He mentioned Charles Reilly, and there was lots of applause. He pointed to Dear Abby, and there was even more applause. Then he pointed to me, and there was an ovation that completely caught me off guard. Afterward, we went to Charles Pierce's dressing room. He came to the door, still in full drag. "GET OUT!" he shouted, pointing his finger at me. "GET OUT! How dare you show up and get more applause than the star of the show!"

The next day, I had a concert, and I needed to get my hair done. I made an appointment at a salon on Rodeo Drive. I was going to take a taxi, but Charles Reilly insisted on driving me. There was no parking space directly in front of the salon, so Charles double-parked while he went around to help me out. The woman driving the car behind him didn't like this at all and started honking her horn like mad. She kept leaning on it while Charles walked around to open the door for me. Finally, she got fed up waiting for him to move, and when there was a break in the other lane, she started to pull out around him.

Charles spun around, shook his fist in the air, and yelled, "HEY, LADY! CAN YOU SING THE LIEBESTOD FROM *TRISTAN UND ISOLDE*? YOU BET YOUR ASS YOU CAN'T!"

In the 1970s, Charles got an idea for a TV series based on my life, which he decided to call *Standing Room Only*. Roberta Peters played an opera singer married to a cop, played by Vincent Gardenia. In the pilot episode, which Charles directed, she's invited to sing at the White House on the same day that her husband has promised his buddies she'll sing at the policeman's ball. They go back and forth, and finally she winds up faking laryngitis and canceling the White House so she can bail out her husband. I never saw it, but it didn't matter, since the network didn't pick it up for the fall season.

In the early '60s, we decided to give up our house on Staten Island and move into Manhattan. The Verazzano Narrows Bridge was being built, and Bob knew it was going to ruin Staten Island, which it did. Also, Robbie was attending Fordham University in the Bronx, and a move to Manhattan would mean a shorter commute for him. We found a co-op in a new building at 175 East Sixty-second Street. I loved being back in Manhattan, but after we were there a few years, the maintenance got so high that Bob had had enough. Even though he was born in New York, he'd never liked the city much, and he decided to look around for a house for us in the country. I didn't want to move, but again, I kept my mouth shut. He did a lot of research and finally settled on New Hampshire because of the low taxes there. Neither of the kids wanted to leave. At Fordham, Robbie was enrolled in the ROTC program, which meant he had to transfer to another school that had ROTC. (Luckily, the University of New Hampshire did.) It was harder for Kathleen, who was about to go into her sophomore year in high school and was very attached to her classmates. I didn't help matters by crying all day when we left Manhattan and drove north to a little town in the middle of nowhere—Londonderry, New Hampshire.

I guess once you get a real taste of New York, it's hard to adjust to living anywhere else. For most of the time we lived in Londonderry, I thought that New Hampshire must be the asshole of America. It was good for Kathleen, though, because she was exposed to a whole new world. We enrolled her in Pinkerton Academy, in Derry, where Robert Frost had taught at one time. Most of the kids who attended the school came from farm families—good, solid, New England folks. Many of them had never been to New York in their lives.

Bob and I had promised Kathleen that one of us would pick her up after school every day at a certain time, and at first, if we were more than five minutes late, she would have a tantrum. She didn't want to spend any more time there than she absolutely had to. She complained all the time about how we'd stuck her in the middle of a bunch of hayseeds just because Daddy wanted lower taxes. She complained that the local kids' idea of a big time was going down and sitting at the A&W. But eventually she got into

Chatting with New York governor
Nelson A. Rockefeller. I look like
I'm complaining about taxes.
Personal collection of Eileen Farrell.

school activities, and after that she loved it. She managed the basketball and softball teams, she was in French Club, she got elected to the State of New Hampshire National Honor Society. All of a sudden, we didn't see her much in the evenings.

One good thing that happened in New Hampshire was that the Catholic Church finally forgave Bob for his first marriage. We attended Mass at St. Jude's, a little country church. I was doing a lot of television in those days, and every time I appeared on some show, the priest would mention it on Sunday morning. I thought he might be willing to help us, so Bob and I went to him and explained our predicament. Things were loosening up in the church around this time, and the priest said, "Don't worry, I'll take care of everything for you." And he did. We were married all over again in the Church and returned to the fold. It was nice to be back.

Even though I had a lot of relatives in Massachusetts and Rhode Island, I felt pretty isolated in New Hampshire. Whenever I had a concert in Manhattan, I had to fly to Manchester and then on to New York in a little Fairchild plane that looked like something out of *Petticoat Junction*. I'm afraid to fly even in the most deluxe plane, and I died a thousand deaths during those commuter flights.

I missed being so far from the center of things. Shortly before we left Sixty-second Street, I had been introduced to Tallulah Bankhead by a mutual friend. We were invited to drinks and dinner at her house, but when we got there, there was no dinner, just plenty of drinks. After we had several rounds, we went to a neighborhood restaurant to get something to eat. Tallulah was pretty well oiled, and during dinner she leaned over to me and said, "My daaaahling, you must give me your new phone number in New Hampshire." About a week after we moved up to Londonderry, I got a telegram from Tallulah, which read, "LOST YOUR PHONE NUMBER STOP PLEASE CALL ME STOP."

I called her and said, "Hi, Tallulah. It's Eileen." And she said, "Oh, my daaaahling, I can't talk to you right now. I'm watching *As the World Turns*. Good-bye."

I hung up. All of a sudden, I felt a million miles from anywhere.

⌒

We had all known for a long time that when Robbie finished his schooling at the University of New Hampshire, he would be drafted to serve in Vietnam. Graduation day came, and it couldn't be avoided any longer. Robbie had always been fascinated by planes, so he went into the Air Force. Bob bought him a new car so he could drive cross-country to Mather Air Force Base near Sacramento, where he'd been assigned. He pulled out of the driveway while we stood waving good-bye, and I cried for the rest of the day, wondering if I'd ever see him again.

Robbie called us at various points on his cross-country trip, and Bob put up a map in the kitchen with little pins in it that he moved, keeping track of Robbie's progress. I don't know why he did it. I guess he was scared of losing him and it made him feel that he had some control over what was happening.

Eventually Robbie went over to Vietnam. The whole time he was there, I said my rosary every single night. I was so frightened that he wouldn't make it back. One summer when he was overseas, the rest of us were up in Maine for our usual retreat. Astrid Mortensen had left us by then, and I had hired a local woman named Nellie Ward as our summertime housekeeper. Nellie had a grandson in Vietnam, and we used to talk sometimes about how much we worried about our boys. One day when Nellie was working in the house, her daughter and son-in-law pulled into our driveway. I was outside, and as soon as they stepped out of the car, I knew from the looks on their faces what had happened. Nellie came out the front door and stood on the porch, and her hands were shaking. "What's wrong?" she asked.

It was terrible. Afterward, I kept thinking, "It could have been Robbie. Someday it might be Robbie."

Robbie went to Vietnam as a navigator bombardier. All told, he was on about twenty-five missions. Of course, in strategic air command everything is a big secret, so he never wrote to us about it, and when he was home on leave, he never mentioned what he did. But I could tell that being in active duty in Vietnam had affected him deeply. Since he had dropped so many bombs, he knew he must have killed many people. One Christmas, when he was home, we were all getting ready to go to Mass, and Robbie said, "I'm not going." And he didn't—not for a long, long time.

My father was in World War I. My brother was in World War II. My son was in Vietnam. That's enough.

In the late '50s, my mother suffered a heart attack, and afterward she always carried nitroglycerine pills in a little holder she wore around her neck.

In 1964, while we were up in Maine getting ready to come home, Robbie had a terrible car accident. We'd had a party, and Robbie was driving one of the guests home. On his way back, he had a head-on collision with another driver. His head went through the windshield, and he needed to have fifty-plus stitches. We got through that, and on August 27, we went back to New York. We'd just gotten to the apartment when the phone rang. It was my Aunt Helen, calling to say that my mother was dead. She'd been perfectly fine, but after lunch that day, she'd felt a little tired and told Aunt Helen she was going to take a nap. She lay down on the bed and died instantly.

I was an orphan now. It was a strange feeling. My mother had, in her quiet way, been the engine that drove me into a singing career in the first place. Everything I had I owed to her and to the fact that she never stopped believing in me. I must have made it pretty hard for her at times, since I was such a rotten student and wasn't really serious about anything. But she thought that my voice was something special, and she never let anyone persuade her otherwise.

She'd been with me for so many great nights in my career, and if she was proud one night and disappointed the next, I didn't know it, because she never tipped her hand. Probably the hardest time between us was after I met Bob, and I think her problems with him had a lot to do with the fact that she was just plain scared of losing me. Again, she never said a word about it. She believed that nothing good could come of getting in a knockdown argument about something, and I'm thankful that some of that has rubbed off on me.

If I'd had a different sort of mother, somebody who pushed me and needed my success to build herself up, I think I might have gotten very wrapped up in myself and my career, and then I really would have had problems along the way. But my mother was the voice of reason. She helped keep me on course. Lucky me.

CHAPTER ELEVEN

DURING the years we were stuck up in New Hampshire, I kept up a busy concert schedule. Several years before, George Trovillo had moved to San Diego, and George Molloy replaced him as my regular accompanist. I did fewer recordings than I had before, but I did get an offer for a Broadway musical—the part of the Marx Brothers' mother in *Minnie's Boys*. I thought it was funny that they thought of a good Irish Catholic girl to play the mother of the Marx Brothers, and after I looked the part over, I decided it wasn't for me. So they got Shelley Winters instead. I never did get around to doing a stage musical, although several years later I was offered the part of Grizabella in *Cats,* and couldn't accept it because of my schedule. I would have loved to do Mama Rose in *Gypsy,* but nobody ever asked me.

In the early 1970s, ABC Records signed me to do a complete recording of Donizetti's *Maria Stuarda,* with my old friend Beverly Sills. I played Elizabeth I, a role that's usually taken by a mezzo, but Edgar Vincent suggested to ABC that it might be interesting to cast a dramatic soprano for once. It was a great part, and I read everything about Elizabeth I could get my hands on. I'd never done a bel canto opera before, and it was awfully difficult to get my voice to move as fast as it needed to. We recorded it in London, and when we weren't working, Beverly and I had a terrific time shopping and going to the theater. Beverly's husband, Peter, and daughter Muffy were with her, along with Roland Gagnon, who wrote all Beverly's cadenzas; Kathleen was with me. I usually avoid sight-seeing altogether when I'm singing, but after Kathleen threatened to have a tantrum, she did manage to get me to the Tower of London for a few minutes.

The sessions were something else. Mary and Elizabeth were challenging roles for both Beverly and me, and we weren't helped at all by the conductor, Aldo Ceccato. His tempos were so slow that I ran out of breath singing Donizetti's intricate lines. One day we were doing a take of a particularly tough section, and Ceccato was dragging along. I ran so short of breath that I thought I was going to pass out. I had my little glass of warm Coca-Cola next to me, and all of a sudden, Ceccato saw what was happening, threw down his baton, and ran over and splashed Coca-Cola in my face!

Beverly and I were supposed to make another recording together. We had done a very successful pair of concerts for the Chamber Music Society of Lincoln Center—duets of Brahms, Schubert, and Schumann—and Angel wanted to put it on vinyl. The contracts were all drawn up, but the head of ABC Records, Beverly's label at the time, wouldn't release her to do the recording, so that was the end of that.

Then, in 1971, I got a call from Wilfred Bain, dean of Indiana University's School of Music. Dean Bain had been at IU since 1947 and had developed quite a distinguished faculty. He wasn't interested in hiring people with twenty-nine different teaching degrees; he wanted top performers who could transmit their experience in a way that the students could really understand. Menachem Pressler and Jorge Bolet taught piano there; Janos Starker, cello; and Margaret Harshaw, voice. Under Dean Bain, IU had built one of the top music schools in the country. Mitch Miller had told him that I might be interested in joining the voice faculty, and Bain had invited me several times in the past, but I had always said no. Now he was asking me again because he needed somebody for the fall 1971 semester.

"What do you think?" I asked Bob. I had never taught in my life, not even an occasional private lesson, and I wasn't quite sure I wanted to do it. But I started to think, why not?

"If you want to go," said Bob, "we'll go."

We went back and forth with Indiana until we came to terms on salary. Since a full teaching schedule would require me to give up a lot of performing, I insisted on getting automatic tenure. We found a spacious split-level house on Meadowbrook Road in Bloomington, only a five-minute drive from the campus, and off we went. Kathy transferred from Emmanuel College and finished up her premed work at the university; after he returned from Vietnam, Robbie entered IU's law school.

My appointment to the IU faculty got quite a bit of publicity. I later found out that lots of people in Bloomington expected me to pull into town in a Lincoln Town Car, and instead I came in a Ford station wagon piled to the ceiling with junk. Bloomington was a pretty town. The Jordan River ran through the middle of it, and there were those beautiful, austere stone buildings everywhere, built from the rock in the nearby quarries. I soon found out that Indiana wasn't meant for a New Englander. The summers were miserable—hot and humid—and we couldn't wait to get out of town at the end of the school year and head up to Maine.

The only thing Bob liked about the heat was that it made for a long growing season, and he immediately put in a huge garden.

He grew his own onions, parsley, and berries, and he was especially proud of his tomatoes. Bob was a marvelous cook, and he'd turn out terrific homemade tomato sauce and jams, fresh from the garden.

He loved to talk about gardening with our across-the-street neighbors, Marge and Bernard Clayton. Bernie had an important career as a photojournalist—he took a famous photo of the Japanese surrendering to Macarthur—and later on he wrote several cookbooks on breads and pastries. He would call us in the afternoon and say, "I just put two kinds of brioche in the oven—come on over and see which one you like best."

Bob also got involved with local politics, so he had a lot to occupy his time. One of my favorite things to do was to go golfing. There was a course near our home, and on Saturday mornings I would go out at seven, before anyone else was out, and play nine holes.

Indiana University's School of Music wasn't just a conservatory—it was also home to the IU Opera Theater, which was, for all intents and purposes, a professional opera company. This made a great recruiting post for talented young students, but it also posed its share of problems. On the very first day of every semester, auditions were held for that year's opera productions. There were six productions staged each year, and I'm not talking about typical "student" operas, like *Amahl and the Night Visitors* or *Gianni Schicchi*. I mean the kind of operas that make you spit blood on the stage, like *Parsifal, Don Carlo,* and *Jenůfa*. There were two separate casts and orchestras for each opera, which meant that we had to listen to a lot of students audition. It took two full days at the beginning of the semester. An opera casting committee, which I later served on, was ultimately responsible for deciding which students sang which part. There were also auditions for private lessons, of course—we were each supposed to take a minimum of eight students, and some teachers got really greedy and took over twenty! I couldn't handle that many students—there's just no time to give them the kind of attention they're paying for—so I tried to keep the number around ten or twelve per semester. A weekly lesson ran for one hour, but I didn't think that meeting once a week was going to be enough. Since we could schedule our lessons any way we pleased, I broke the hour up into two half-hours a week. It was much easier to monitor their progress that way, and we got a lot more accomplished, and got to know each other better.

I worked four days a week, and I worked hard. I generally started around nine o'clock in the morning and went until about half past three in the afternoon. It was a long day, and I found that I was exhausted by the end of it: You give so much of yourself trying to get students to put energy into their singing that at the end of the day, you don't have a whole lot left over for yourself. There was a lot of activity at IU: All the freshmen had to sing at the end of the semester, and juniors and seniors had to give full end-of-the-year recitals, to say nothing of all the performances required of the masters and doctoral students. On top of that, you'd be expected to sit in on opera rehearsals if your students were in the cast, to correct their mistakes and cheer them on. And there were always little chamber music and orchestra concerts on campus, just about any night of the week.

It was a great atmosphere for soaking up music, and if you were talented, ambitious, and hard-working, you could get a terrific start at IU. I loved being with the kids, and lots of them called me "Mom." One of my favorites was a very talented dramatic mezzo named Diann Thomas, who became a close friend of Kathleen's. Diann was a natural-born performer who went on to a nice career in regional opera and summer stock; she's also been lucky to have a wonderful husband, Steve Harris. I gave Diann tips on everything from how to sing Verdi to how to make a marinade for chicken out of onion soup mix, apricot preserves, and Catalina salad dressing.

The first couple of years passed without any big problems, although Bob did begin to resent how much of my time teaching took up, just as he had resented the fact that singing took me away from him. I loved the challenge of trying to help the students. There were so many talented young singers at IU, but many of them had some basic problems that needed lots of work. For one thing, most of them just got up and sang, without paying attention to the words. I tried to teach them all of Miss Mac's tricks, getting them to focus on the text and put meaning into what they were singing. Another problem was that very few of them sounded like themselves. They had come up with some manufactured sound that they thought was going to make a big impression, and I had to struggle to get them to sing in their natural voices.

I also worked with them on making sure breathing and the words were always coordinated; when you play around with the text, it mustn't interfere with the breathing. I tried to get them to realize that the voice doesn't go up and down—it goes out. You can't compare a voice to a piano keyboard; the way the voice moves is so different from any other instrument. In addition to helping with technique and style, I tried to get across some idea of what being a working singer was all about.

I had lots of good students during my nine years at Bloomington. I'll always remember one lovely girl, Sue Anne Gershenson. Sue Anne's mother had died several years earlier, and she was still having an awfully hard time dealing with it. Sue Anne was a freshman, and very shy. She came to IU at the same time I did. One day, as I was getting settled in my office, she came by and knocked on the door. "Excuse me," she said, very timidly. "Do you teach freshmen?"

"Well, I don't really know whether I teach freshmen or not,"

Giving pointers to one of my
students, Lynelle Frankforter, at an
Indiana University opera rehearsal.
Personal collection of Eileen Farrell.

I responded. "I've never taught before. Why don't you come in and sing for me and I'll let you know?"

She sang "My Man's Gone Now" from *Porgy and Bess,* and I couldn't believe such a big voice was coming out of such a little girl. I accepted her as a student, and she worked hard and did very well. I remember one day when she came in terribly upset and depressed. She sat down at the piano, as if in a daze. I knew she was thinking about her mother and how much she missed her. I said, "Just put it in the music, Sue Anne." And she did.

Later on, Sue Anne was quite successful in musical theater—she even got a small part in Stephen Sondheim's *Sunday in the Park with George* on Broadway.

Then there was Sunny Joy Langton. She was a lovely young lyric soprano who had had some coachings with George Trovillo out in San Diego, and he had suggested that she study with me. At her first lesson, Sunny Joy didn't do very well. I stopped her and said, "You seem very nervous."

"Oh, yes, Miss Farrell," she said, "I'm terribly nervous."

"Why should you be nervous in front of me?" I asked.

"Well, Miss Farrell," said Sunny Joy, "after all—you used to be a star."

I nearly came apart. Right away it got around, and one of my doctoral students went out and had a T-shirt specially printed up with I USED TO BE A STAR in big block letters.

During the year I was busy with my teaching schedule, and in the summer we left for Maine, so I didn't have much time for socializing with faculty members. I liked several people in the school—Martha Lipton, Gianna D'Angelo, and Roger Havranek, who was head of the voice department. I'd sung with Martha years before, and was fond of her. For a long time we had a regular Wednesday night date to go to Weight Watchers together. I worked hard at it and lost over thirty pounds at one point, but Martha cheated like crazy. The morning after a meeting, I would catch her sneaking in the back entrance of the music building carrying a bag of doughnuts. The voice department also included Virginia MacWatters, who had sung lots of Adeles (in *Fledermaus*) at the Met once upon a time and trotted around campus in her miniskirts and white go-go boots. And there was Camilla Williams, who had the most amazing collection of outfits I ever saw anybody wear on campus, including a pair of mink pants. Camilla also had a special way of rewarding her students if they had a good lesson: She'd give them a quarter.

But the queen bee of the voice department was Margaret Harshaw. I'm not sure I'd seen her since I wrecked our *Aida* duet on my radio show. From the day I arrived, Margaret let it be known that she wasn't happy about my presence on her turf. A lot of people have said that we feuded, but we never did. Most of the time, Margaret wouldn't speak to me. I have no idea what her problem was—maybe she felt threatened, although I don't know why she would have—her reputation as a teacher was secure and, anyway, I didn't have the least interest in competing with her. Maybe it was the fact that her teaching career had actually over-shadowed her performing career, and I was still singing as often as I could. Whatever her problem was, she was very territorial. We would meet each other in the hall. I'd say, "Good morning, Margaret," and she would sort of stiffen and look in the other di-rection. It probably wasn't in the cards for us to be good friends—we were such completely different types of people. Margaret liked to play the diva on campus. I would say that intimidation was probably a big factor in her teaching. She was always very imposing and aloof—as if she wanted to remind you, in case you forgot, that she had a special place in the grand scheme of things. She didn't drive to campus herself—she usually conned one of her students into picking her up in the morning and driving her back at night.

For the first couple of years, I felt my way along and didn't make any trouble. But after a while I realized there was something very wrong about the way the students were pushed into opera productions. No junior in college should be shoved into *Arabella,* for God's sake! At the beginning of the year, you might hear a promising singer with a nice, healthy voice auditioning. Two years later, the same singer would give a recital, and you would sit there and ask yourself what had happened. I remember one young soprano with a nice voice who had the bad luck to get cast as Elisabetta in *Don Carlo*—and by the time she left Bloomington, she had a wobble that you could have driven a herd of cattle through.

One year, when I was on the casting committee, there was a big push to cast Sunny Joy Langton as Gilda in *Rigoletto.* I wouldn't stand for it. I told the others on the committee there was no way Sunny Joy was ready for a part like that. None of them liked that much—especially Sunny Joy, until she took a good look at the score and realized I was right.

One problem with the whole setup at Bloomington was that the university planned the season in advance, as a kind of recruiting tool for students, before they knew what singers they had available. If they had done the whole thing in reverse, choosing the operas based on the singers who were on campus, everyone would have been much better off. I started speaking up about this practice of shoving singers into roles before they were ready, and I'm afraid it didn't do much to endear me to my colleagues—especially Margaret.

Too many people on the faculty seemed to be on a huge ego trip. For them, teaching wasn't about developing young voices and sending them out into the world. Their entire sense of accomplishment was confined to what happened on the Bloomington campus—the more students in opera productions, the better. Once, at a rehearsal, a colleague turned to me and said, "I have *four* students in this one. How many do *you* have?" I think most of them thought I was a little strange. In my office I had a sign up that said, HELP STAMP OUT OPERA. I can just imagine how Margaret must have loved *that*.

I'd been teaching at IU for about three years when some of my students started asking me about teaching a jazz course. Several of them had gotten hold of the records I'd done with Luther Henderson and André Previn, and they said they wanted to learn how to sing pop as well as opera. IU had a good jazz department, headed by Dave Baker, but there was no voice class.

In those days, if you wanted to introduce a class to the IU curriculum, you had to make a formal proposal before the entire music faculty. I worked up a plan for a jazz singing class that I thought was pretty good, and I made my presentation. After I finished, everyone just looked at me. Nobody said a word. Finally, Virginia MacWatters cleared her throat and said, "Well, tell me something—who would teach this class?"

"*I* would, Virginia."

More silence. I thought the whole thing had bombed, but Charles Webb, who had taken Wilfred Bain's place as dean, was behind it all the way, so it passed. The jazz class started the following year, and it turned out to be one of the most popular courses the department had ever had. Students were elbowing each other out of the way to get into it. I started with only fifteen students. They had to audition, and lots of the ones I took were from the theater department.

I knew I would have to be careful about how I handled the voice majors who studied with other people, so in the jazz class, I didn't do much with the voice itself. I approached jazz in a fairly structured way, showing students how to keep good breath support even though they were singing numbers that flew all over the place. I figured that once they got the basics down, they could allow themselves to have a lot of freedom. I spent a lot of time on rhythm, and I showed them how to interpolate high notes and straighten tones and bend pitches in order to get the song's message across. I showed them how to sing with a microphone. Most of all, I worked on phrasing and the correct pronunciation and coloring of words—just as important, if not more so, than in opera singing.

I also included a section on scat singing. I had two wonderful pianists who played for my classes—Joey Singer and Kenny Greenhouse. Kenny played for my scat lessons; he would improvise while I circled the room and pointed to the students, who would stand up and start singing scat. It was a great way of helping them learn to listen to what was around them instead of to themselves. By the end of the semester, most of them had a pretty good idea of what improvising was all about.

I knew I couldn't give my jazz students a test at the end of the year, so I decided to put on a cabaret evening in the campus recital hall, which was perfect because it had a low stage. We got Joey Singer to play, along with a bass player and drummer. My students would tell Joey which numbers they were going to sing, and he would write out the charts for them. I put a bunch of stools on the stage, asked the boys to wear tuxes and the girls long evening dresses, and away they went. It was such a smash that after a few seasons, we had to move into the opera house, which had a lot more seats. To close the evening, I'd come out and sing "Come Rain or Come Shine" or some other number.

The jazz class really snowballed over the years. I was thrilled that it was so popular, but by the late seventies, things were changing for me at IU. I still liked teaching, but it was getting increasingly hard to justify staying on. More and more promising voices were being wrecked, and no one on the faculty seemed to care. I didn't have the same respect for Charles Webb that I had for Wilfred Bain, I was getting in more fights on the casting committee, and my blood pressure was going through the roof. I was starting to think that IU wasn't the place for me, after all.

In 1980 I recorded the duet "For the Good Times" with Frank Sinatra for his *Trilogy* album. It got a lot of attention, and I was starting to think I might like to do less teaching and more performing. Around the same time, I paid a visit to my doctor, and my systolic pressure was up around 180. "I think maybe it's time you got out of there," he said, and I decided maybe he was right.

Then everything really went to hell. I gave an interview to United Press International (UPI), followed by one to the IU *Daily Student*. In both, I said that I was getting fed up with the way students were treated like second-class citizens. When they were published, lots of people in the music school were furious. Some time earlier, I had been named a Distinguished Professor, the university's top faculty honor. There was a meeting scheduled of the music school's Distinguished Professors (Menachem Pressler, Janor Starker, Harvey Phillips, and me), and when the UPI interview came out, I received a call saying that the meeting had suddenly been canceled. I realized then and there that I was probably going to be given the cold shoulder in the department, and no doubt my job would be even tougher from now on. Even though it was the middle of the semester, I decided I'd better pack up and leave. I went home and talked it over with Bob. "I think it's time for me to go," I said. He was delighted, since he'd been jealous of how much time teaching kept me away from home.

Bob said he would speak to Charles Webb for me. I was teaching a student in my studio when I heard the click-click-click of Charles's shoes coming down the hall.

"Would you please excuse us for a moment?" he asked my

student, "I must speak with Miss Farrell right away." The student ducked out, and Charles turned to me.

"Bob just came to me and told me the news. You can't do this. It's the middle of the semester.

"I don't want to do it, Charles," I said. "But I have to. I can't stand what's going on at the school."

"Well, Eileen, what can I do?" asked Charles. "I can't give you any more money, because you're already making more than anybody else in the school."

I resisted the temptation to say "Bullshit!" Charles just didn't understand. They could have doubled my salary and I still wouldn't have wanted to stay. I didn't feel I *could* stay, even for one more month. My health was at stake—I was already up to six Tylenols a day.

As soon as the announcement was made, the *Today* show covered it with a big story, headlined, "Farrell Is Leaving." That really made my pals in the music school mad, and Janos Starker sat down and wrote a letter to the *Daily Student* accusing me of staging the whole thing just for the publicity.

That was it. Bob asked me where I wanted to live—he was open to anything except New York City—and I said, "Maine." We sold the house in Indiana and headed back to New England. My Hoosier days were finished.

CHAPTER TWELVE

WHILE I WAS still teaching at Indiana University, I was booked for a recital at Hunter College in New York City. I was in the middle of the program when I suddenly thought, "Why in the hell am I doing this? This is a lot of hard work." At the end of the first half, I came offstage and said to Bob and Herbert Barrett, "I've got news for you. This is my last recital." Barrett looked like someone had hit him between the eyes with a two-by-four.

"You mean it?" said Bob.

"Absolutely," I said. "I'll still do orchestra engagements. But with teaching full-time, I just can't concentrate on preparing a recital anymore. It's too much."

It was that simple—I just knew, then and there, that I was finished with one more phase of my career. Some people can't stop. Roberta Peters is such a workaholic that she'll probably go on until she drops. Jan Peerce couldn't have stopped for anything in the world: I remember how at the end of his life, he was

singing operas while he was leaning on a cane. I loved singing—
but I never felt I would die if I didn't sing.

A couple of years before we left Indiana, we had sold our summer house on Moosehead Lake, so before we could take up res-
idence in Maine, we had to go house hunting. We found a large
four-bedroom, five-bathroom house in Castine. Quite a few retired people lived there, and it was the kind of place where
people do a lot of entertaining and visiting back and forth, so
Bob and I had a pretty active social life.

I liked being back in Maine, and for a while I kept my
hand in teaching, giving master classes at the Peabody Institute and the University of Maine at Orono. Most of the time,
though, I felt more like a housewife than a diva. Once, our
golden retriever, Brandy, tangled with a skunk. Bob wouldn't
go near her, so it was up to me, and I tried giving her a bath
in tomato juice. That didn't work, so I called a friend, who
told me that the best way to get the smell off her was to bathe
her with a douche. I went right down to the local drugstore
and bought seven or eight boxes of Massengill—after all, she
was a big dog. The clerk rang it up, and as she handed me the
bag, she gave me a big smile and said, "Have a nice evening,
Miss Farrell."

One of the best parts about living in Maine was meeting my
great friend Esther Rauch. One day I was at the hairdresser and
there was a lady reading something as she sat under the dryer. All
of a sudden she burst out laughing, so I asked her what was so
funny. It was the start of one of the most important friendships of
my life. Esther is a brilliant woman, with a marvelous sense of humor. At college, she studied seventeenth-century English literature, and when I met her she was vice-president of the Bangor
Seminary. Bob was very fond of her and her husband, Chick, a

retired admiral. (Bob figured that anyone who had been captain of a nuclear submarine couldn't be all bad.)

Esther and I started spending a lot of time together. We cooked together (Bob and I showed Esther how to bake bread), went shopping, and went out to lunch and laughed so hard that we usually emptied our section. We'd go to Esther and Chick's summer cottage and watch the sun set over Penobscot Bay. Esther and I talked about everything, especially music. One day she told me that she didn't like Wagner. "That's because you don't know how to listen to it," I said. So we got together every week for a while, and I would play records and explain to Esther about the motifs and what to listen for, taking her through it step by step. Esther's friendship was a great gift in my life. During my years of keeping up a busy work schedule, I hadn't had much time to develop women friends, and of course, I always had to worry about Bob being jealous. But even he had to admit that Esther was really something.

When Robbie got off active duty in Vietnam, he stayed in the reserves and used the GI bill to go to law school at Indiana University. After that, he went back on active duty, but a short time later he collapsed a lung. He was in so much pain that he was sent home to recuperate. After he recovered, he entered the University of Maine. He got his MBA there, and went on to teach economics and maritime law at the Maine Maritime Academy. Some time later he started practicing law.

Kathleen was thriving. She'd gotten her AB from Indiana University and stayed on there to attend medical school. After that, she went to the Maine Medical Center, in Portland, where she did a two-year psychology residency. She came home with some pretty wild stories. My favorite was the one about the night she was on duty at the hospital and a patient was brought in. This woman was pretty much out of it, and when Kathleen asked her what her name was, she said, "My name is Eileen Farrell. Everyone says we look just alike, but the other one is *much* fatter than I am." After a couple of years, Kathleen decided psych wasn't for her after all, and she switched to radiology. She was at the Lahey Clinic in Burlington, Massachusetts, for three years, then got a fellowship in cardiovascular/interventional radiology at Brigham and Women's Hospital in Boston, where she later joined the staff. Bob and I were very proud of both of our kids.

The day after we moved to Castine, I was unpacking and putting things away, and all of a sudden, I couldn't stand up. It turned out I had torn cartilage in my knee. I had surgery for it, which didn't go too well, and I was still in a lot of discomfort by the time I was scheduled to start singing again. One of the first things I did after my surgery was Beverly Sills's farewell gala at the New York State Theater. I wasn't feeling up to it at all, but Beverly and I had been good friends for a long time, and I wouldn't have dreamed of canceling.

Her farewell was a performance of *Die Fledermaus,* with Beverly as Rosalinde. In the second-act party scene, Kitty Carlisle played Prince Orlofsky, and there was a wonderful lineup of party guests—all good friends of Beverly's—who would each do a turn. Carol Burnett was the emcee, and after her came Dinah Shore, Leontyne Price, Renata Scotto, Donald Gramm, Ethel Merman, Mary Martin, and lots of others. I was scheduled to sing "I've Got the World on a String," accompanied by Bobby Short. I showed up at the State Theater on the day of the performance, and went straight to the dressing room. There was limited space at the theater, and I had two roommates in my dressing room— Marty Martin and Ethel Merman. Mary came with a hairdresser, and she sat there worrying about her hair and costume and makeup, talking nonstop the entire time. Ethel showed up in her dress with her hair already done and planted herself in a chair to watch *Fledermaus* on the TV monitor they'd set up for us. She sat there with her hands folded across her stomach, watching it for a long time with kind of a puzzled look on her face. She made it through Kitty Carlisle singing "Chacun à son goût." Finally she turned to me and snapped, in that famous voice, "HOW LONG IS THIS THING GOING TO LAST?"

"I don't know, Ethel," I said.

"WHADDYA MEAN, YOU DON'T KNOW? CHRIST ALMIGHTY, YOU SING OPERA, DON'T YOU? YOU SHOULD KNOW!"

I continued to get ready, but I could hardly concentrate because every so often, Ethel would break out with, "*WHEN* IS THIS DAMNED THING GOING TO END? OH, SHIT, THIS IS *TERRIBLE!*"

Bobby and I did our number, which was tough for me because I couldn't bend my knee at all. Then we sat down on the stage to listen to Renata Scotto sing "Over the Rainbow." Now, *that* was some performance. Scotto was a marvelous opera singer, but if ever there was an argument against what everybody these days calls "crossover," this was it. Bobby and I sat in amazement while Scotto opened her eyes very wide and sang, "When happy little bluebirds fly . . ." like it was the last gasp of Suor Angelica.

"Oh, God," said Bobby. "Here come the bluebirds!" And I had to beg him to stop, or I knew we'd both be kicked out.

In 1982, the Kool Jazz Festival invited me to sing a joint concert with Mabel Mercer at Lincoln Center's Alice Tully Hall. It was great to see Mabel again, but right away, I could tell she was nervous about doing this concert, because she hadn't appeared onstage in several years. Her voice wasn't what it had been, and at rehearsal she got upset because she really had very few solid notes left. She'd try and try, but she couldn't quite do what she wanted to do. She knew the concert was sold out, and she was terrified that she was going to disappoint all her fans.

"I don't sound good at all," she said.

"Cut it out, Mabel," I said. "You're getting all tense. Just do what you've always done and it's going to come out fine."

With Mabel Mercer, before our
Kool Jazz Festival concert at Lincoln
Center in the early '80s. I'm usually
against the idea of pirate tapes, but I
would *love* to have a souvenir of that
evening. Personal collection of
Eileen Farrell.

Which was what happened. Alice Tully Hall was packed to the rafters that night. Mabel had always sat when she sang, so I sat alongside her. Her eyes were quite bad by this point, and I had made a huge spiral notebook with all the lyrics of every song. I wrote her lines in black, in big block letters on the left-hand side of the book, so she could see them, and mine in red on the right-hand side. We did "Chase Me, Charlie, over the Garden Wall," a couple of beautiful songs from *The Yearling,* a few from *Stop the World—I Want to Get Off.* Loonis McGlohon and his band played for us. Mabel was so unsteady on her feet that when we took bows at intermission, I had to hold onto her. But she delivered that night, just as she always had. The crowd gave us one ovation after another, and minute by minute, I could feel Mabel's confidence coming back. At the very end, she got so excited by the audience's reaction that she did a little buck and wing as she went off, and I had no choice but to follow along. I usually am against the whole idea of pirate recordings, but I have to admit, I'd love to have a tape of that night. Somebody out there must have one.

In 1986, Bob had a routine exam that showed a spot on his lungs. Kathleen discussed it with several of her colleagues, who felt that surgery was the way to go so we could find out exactly what it was. I had been hospitalized myself for a few days at the Lahey Clinic for some minor surgery, and the day I was released, Bob was admitted to New England Deaconess. They removed a malignant lump, and everyone thought the operation was a success. After nine days in the hospital, he seemed to be making a steady recovery, and he went to Kathleen's house in Boston to finish recuperating. After two days, he got much worse and was sent back to the hospital. It turned out he had a pulmonary infarction, and he would up in the intensive care unit.

Bob lost ground day by day. I went to visit him often, but I was allowed to stay in the unit only five minutes at a time. On a

Saturday night, about two weeks after he'd been readmitted, I went in to see him. He was hooked up to seven different tubes, and his hands were tied with bandages so he wouldn't move around too much. He was playing the little radio that Shirley Cowell had given me. When I came into the room and leaned over the bed, he made a gesture for me to cut off the bandages on his wrists.

"Daddy," I said, "I can't do that without asking the nurse." He raised his arm high enough to shake his fist at me.

On the way out that night, Kathleen said, "If he does get better, he'll probably have to be on an oxygen tank all the time."

I knew that would never do for Bob Reagan; I knew he'd rather die right now than be a semi-invalid for the rest of his life. That night, Kathleen and I went to Mass, and I prayed for God to take him and not let him linger. At two o'clock that morning Kathleen got a call to come to the hospital—the strain on his heart was too much, and he was slipping fast. By the time she got there, Bob had died of heart failure. It was Mother's Day 1986.

I'll always be grateful to our good friends Al Bagot and Carol Badgley, who contacted our priest and made all the funeral arrangements. The week after Bob was buried, I had to reenter the hospital for colon surgery. All the nurses said, "How's Mr. Reagan? Is Mr. Reagan coming in to see you?"

I missed Bob terribly. There had been many rough spots along the way. His possessiveness had caused a lot of tension in our marriage, but he had been a good husband and a great father. It's true that he meddled in my career to a certain extent. He never felt comfortable around musicians, and a lot of times he put his two cents in just to exert a little more control over me. But he also made some tremendous business decisions that are still benefiting me today. And most of the time, when he did get involved in my career, I honestly believe it was because he thought that I deserved the very best, and he knew I couldn't be counted on to ask for it myself. He wanted everyone to show respect for me. Sometimes he made me feel as if I was his own personal property, but I never once doubted that he believed in me. Bob had loved music so much, and there were so many songs that reminded me of him. I couldn't even think about opening my mouth to sing, and in my worst moments, I figured I'd probably never work again.

Later that year I sold our house in Castine and bought a condominium in Yarmouth, about ten miles north of Portland. I couldn't get there fast enough. The house in Castine seemed three times as big as it had when Bob was there, and at night I couldn't bear being there alone. Our golden retriever, Brandy, used to sleep in between us. From the day that Bob left for the hospital, Brandy refused to get on the bed. She lay by the front door with her head on the sill and waited and waited for him to come home.

I liked Yarmouth. I was closer to the center of things, and used to go in to Portland for performances quite a bit. Even before Bob died, performing had been getting harder and harder for me. I started having terrible panic attacks right before I was about to go onstage. The first one happened at the Kennedy Center right before I was about to sing with the National Symphony. I was backstage, and all of a sudden I thought, "I can't go on." A little while later, in Charlotte, North Carolina, I had to give a speech, and as I was walking onstage, my legs felt like they were going to give way underneath me. My voice started to quaver, and the audience became a blur. God knows I like to talk, but all of a sudden I was tongue-tied and didn't have any idea how I was going to end the speech. From then on, my stage fright just got worse and worse, and the funny thing is that I never did figure out where it came from. Why, all of a sudden, after forty years of performing, would I be so scared I could hardly open my mouth? I'm just happy I don't have to worry about it anymore.

In the mideighties, I hosted a National Public Radio program called *American Popular Singers,* produced by Loonis McGlohon. A few years earlier, Loonis and Alec Wilder, who were very close friends, had put together a radio series called *American Popular Song,* which focused on a string of great American composers, and they had asked me to appear on it. Bob was dead set against it, so I said no. After Bob died, Loonis called to tell me he was producing *American Popular Singers* and asked me if I would be the series host. I was happy to do it. The format for the show was simple: I would talk with a famous American singer for a few minutes, and the guest would sing four or five numbers. At the end, I would join the guest for a duet. We had some wonderful singers on the program—Mabel Mercer, Barbara Cook, Maxine Sullivan, Joe Williams, Bobby Short, Singers Unlimited, and lots of others. All together, we did thirteen hour-long episodes. The one that sticks in my mind most is Mabel's. With just a piano accompaniment, she recited "Ballad of the Harp Weaver." It was a story about a poor little boy who didn't have anything to wear to a party, so his mother stayed up all night sewing something for him and died while she was doing it. Everyone in the studio was dead quiet. I started to cry, which was terrible, because as soon as she finished, I had to start talking to her. She ended the story, and I whispered, "Jesus." You can hear it on the tape. What a spellbinder Mabel was.

Around this time, Margaret Whiting called me. I hadn't seen her in a while, and she said, "Listen, Eileen, what the hell are you doing up there in Maine all by yourself? You need to come down to New York and start working!" I said the same thing that I had said years before when people asked me why I wasn't singing at the Met: "Nobody asked me." After all, a lady—an old lady even more so—likes to be asked. Loonis and Nan McGlohon were egging me on, too, trying to get me back to work so I could get my mind off my troubles. Finally Loonis talked me into doing a record with him and his ensemble for Audiophile Recordings. It was a collection of pop songs that included "Since I Fell for You," "Some Other Time," and a couple of Loonis's own songs. The recording was called *Eileen Farrell—With Much Love*. It was very hard to go back to singing all those sad, wonderful songs so soon after Bob had died. One of the numbers on the record was a medley of "When the World Was Young" and "Once Upon a Summertime." I sang the first lines of "When the World Was Young"—"Ah, the apple trees/And the hive of bees"—and I knew it was going to be rough. By the time I got to the end of the song, I was in tears. The record turned out OK, and one day in 1988, I got a letter from a young fellow named J. Tamblyn Henderson, Jr., who was a producer at a company called Reference Recordings, out in San Francisco. Reference was a small label, but they had been in business for a few years and were getting on solid ground. Tam had been a fan of mine since he was a kid, and he later told me that my recording of "To This We've Come" had changed his life. He asked me to make one more record, with him, "for me and all your devoted fans."

This was laying it on a little thick, but I figured, I'm sitting up here in Maine, not doing a damned thing. So I telephoned him and said, "I'd be happy to make a record for you. What would you like me to sing?" He said later that he practically had to pick himself up off the floor—he had assumed it would be hard to talk me into it. We settled on not one but two recordings, one of songs by my old friend Harold Arlen, and one of Rodgers and Hart tunes. I made several trips down to Charlotte to pick out the songs with Loonis McGlohon. We would hash out which songs we were going to use, and which keys were best for me. I would stay a few days with Loonis and Nan, and Loonis and I would go over the vocal arrangements in his studio, and eventually he would do the charts for all the musicians. By this time I was in my late sixties, and it was hard work getting back in shape, but in time, it came together. While we were cutting the Arlen album, I fell in love with the trumpet playing of Joe Wilder. We decided on the spur of the moment to add "Happiness Is Just a Thing Called Joe," which hadn't been on the original list of Arlen songs we were set to record. We didn't have an arrangement; Joe and I just winged it, and we got the song down in one take. It was great to be working again. Tam Henderson had a terrific engineer, "Professor" Johnson, whose microphones were like nothing I'd ever seen—one of them looked like the heating element in my oven. The first few recordings got a fair amount of attention in the press. The Harold Arlen disk made *Billboard*'s crossover chart, and Tam was encouraged enough to sign me up for several more recordings: We did one of torch songs, one of Alec Wilder's music, and one of songs by Johnny Mercer.

For quite a long time I had been a big fan of the British conductor-arranger Robert Farnon. One day I said to Shirley Cowell, "Before I die, I'd like to make a record with Robert Farnon." She said, "Well, why don't you?" and put up the money for us to make *This Time It's Love*. (When Margaret Whiting found out I was going to be doing the recordings with Robert, she said, "You mean you're working with *God?*") All together, we did four recordings. Loonis and I would work out what we wanted to do and send a tape, with just piano accompaniment, over to Robert in England. He would sit down and write the orchestrations, then I would fly over to England, go into a recording studio, and do the songs for Robert so he could see how I wanted to phrase everything. We'd put that on tape, and I would bring it back to Maine with me and play it every day for a couple of months until I had the orchestrations under my belt. Then, when I was ready, Robert would come over and we would go to a studio, either in California or down in Miami, and record the whole thing.

Robert's musicians were the cream of the crop. Several things I got in one take because I had familiarized myself with

With CBS's Charles Kuralt
and Marilyn Horne at a party to
launch my 1993 recording, *Here*.
Photograph copyright Anita and
Steve Shevett.

everything the orchestra was doing. On *It's Over,* the second album I did with Robert, I got to sing Billy Strayhorn's "Lush Life." It's a great song, and one of the toughest ones ever written, and I worked and worked on it. The melody is difficult and the intervals are tricky—you have to get right on top of those notes. And you have to watch how you handle the words, too—those are "distingué traces," not "distant, gray traces." I was thrilled when we got a good take of it. Robert got a Grammy nomination for his arrangements on this disk.

I always wondered whether I'd know when I no longer sang well. I was pretty sure that my 1995 disk with Robert, *Love Is Letting Go,* would be my last record—after all, you have to quit some time—and the sessions clinched it. I had a hard time staying on pitch. Robert was in the control booth, and whenever I started to go flat, he would subtly point his finger upward a little bit. I was losing my breath support, and if I had a sustained note, the pitch would start to go as my breath went out. Loonis was after me to make one more recording, but I said no. My last live performance anywhere was at a cabaret evening at the Russian Tea Room, put on by the Johnny Mercer Foundation to benefit the Eugene O'Neill School. Margaret Whiting and her husband, Jack Wrangler, asked me to do Johnny's wonderful song "You Grow Sweeter as the Years Go By." I had a hell of a time memorizing it, and I was disgusted with myself when I had to give up and use the music for the performance. Afterward, I said to Margaret and Jack, "That's it. I'm never going to perform again."

"Oh, no, darling," said Margaret. "You'll do other things."

"No, that's it," I said. "I don't want to be creaking around and not up to my form." And I've been true to my word.

In 1992 I moved again. I'd had hip replacement surgery, and I couldn't negotiate the stairs in my Yarmouth condominium any longer. For the past few years, Kathleen had been working at

Georgetown Hospital, but she had just taken a position with the radiology department of Columbia-Presbyterian Hospital in New York. I decided to move, too, to be closer to her. She settled in Washington Township, New Jersey, just across the George Washington Bridge from the hospital, and I found a nice apartment not far from her, with a great view of Riverside Church and upper Manhattan.

I was slowing down, getting older. There's no point in fighting it—it's like complaining about the rain. Since I've officially retired, I've tried to spend as much time with old friends as possible. Two of the best are Esther Rauch and Carol Badgley. For several years, I spent the winter with Carol down at her place in Eleuthera, in the Caribbean, until the cold weather passed. I also stayed in close touch with Diann Thomas, my ex-student from Bloomington, and her husband, Steve Harris. And I saw quite a bit of my show business friends. There was nothing I liked better than to drive in to Manhattan and go to Rainbow and Stars or the Algonquin or the Ballroom, and catch Barbara Cook, Rosemary Clooney, Annie Ross, Maggie Whiting, Lena Horne, Sylvia Syms, and Marlene Verplanck. One of the best cabaret singers around now is Weslia Whitfield—marvelous phrasing and style. I tried to see her every time she played New York.

On February 12, 1992, one night before my seventy-second birthday, I went out to dinner in New York with Sylvia Syms and Rex Reed. We went up to the third floor of the Friars Club, and there was a closed set of double doors. In her funny little voice, Sylvia said, "Are we gonna be in this room?" And she knocked on the door and called out, "HELLO? IS ANYBODY THERE?" I thought she was nuts, but all of a sudden she threw open the doors and the room was full of people singing "Happy Birthday" to me. Shirley Cowell had decided she wanted to throw a party for me, and she'd gotten Sylvia to help her organize it. Maggie Whiting was there, and Gloria De Haven and Barbara Carroll and Bobby Short and Jule Styne and my friend and publicist Helene Greece—all kinds of wonderful people. It was the nicest party I'd ever been to, and I wasn't even dressed for it.

One thing I *don't* do is go to the opera. Someone asked me recently when was the last time I'd been to the Met. I had to be honest and say, "The night I sang my last performance there." To this day, I've never seen the inside of the new Met.

CHAPTER THIRTEEN

NTERVIEWERS used to ask me, "Now that you've done just about everything you could have done in music, what would you like to spend the rest of your life doing?" And I'd say, "I'd like to spend the rest of my life drinking and smoking." I never was much of a drinker, but at the end of every season, as I was getting ready to head up to Maine for my vacation, I'd buy a pack of cigarettes. I'd light one up and in just a few seconds, I'd be hacking and wheezing. So my wish never did come true.

If I were asked today what I'd like to spend the rest of my life doing, I know what I'd say: "Absolutely nothing." My days pass pretty quietly now. I read *The New York Times* from front to back every morning, and I'm always in the middle of some biography or other—often it's one about somebody I worked with. I'm hooked on the radio. It's on all day, and I even listen to it at night when I'm going to sleep—music and talk shows, both. Kathleen is close by, and hardly a day passes that I don't get a phone call from an old friend. Lots of peace and quiet—the kind of retirement everybody should be lucky enough to have.

Every now and then, someone asks me what I think of the state of singing today. I have to rely mostly on what I hear on records, radio, and TV, but I would say that the one thing that many young singers are missing today is an individual personality. With any big star, you should be able to play "drop the needle" and know exactly who's singing, and with too many of the ones today, you can't. I don't know exactly why this is, but I think it may have something to do with training. At Indiana University, I used to hear teachers say things like, "Boy, could I make a terrific mezzo out of that soprano!" What a hell of a thing to say! The most important thing a singer can do is to be true to his own voice, and too many teachers today train the individual sound right out of their students and replace it with something phony and artificial. I was lucky—my teachers never pushed me to sound like anybody but myself.

On the other hand, I think singing is better right now than it's been for a long time. When you've got Deborah Voigt, Bryn Terfel, Renée Fleming, and Sumi Jo, what have you got to complain about? As singers, the kids today are probably much better than most of us were. They're smarter, more curious—they know more than we did. And they've *got* to be smart because there are a lot more opportunities now, and more pressure to go with it. The record labels and the media push and push and try to make stars out of kids who are still feeling their way. Every time someone like Cecilia Bartoli steps outside, a TV camera follows her. The tough ones stay with it and don't let it swallow them up, but it's rough for the others who aren't strong enough. One thing young singers have to remember: All these people who are flattering them, the managers and record producers and conductors, just want to get their project going and make money off it. Nobody will care if these singers lose their voices in the process. There will always be someone else coming along to take their place.

All told, I'm glad my career happened when it did. When I was young and didn't have the faintest idea what I was doing, I was put in the best hands possible. I owe so much to Jimmie Fassett and Lucile Singleton, to Charlie Baker and Miss Mac, to Leopold Stokowski and all the other conductors who were so kind to me at the start, and of course to my mother and father—they all helped me from losing my way.

I had a funny career. Because I had all those people making things so much easier for me, I never felt the struggle that most singers do. If I'd had to fight more to be recognized, I might have had an entirely different approach to singing. Emily Coleman, my old friend who was the music editor at *Newsweek* for many years, once said that Dorothy Kirsten never had time to sleep because she was too busy scheming. I was never that way. I just glided along from one thing to another, hardly thinking about where or how fast I was going. I was never greedy for more. Maybe if it had been harder for me at the beginning, I might have done a lot more elbowing later on and hung in there longer. I might have tried to finesse things with Rudolf Bing instead of telling him to go to hell.

In some ways, I'm not sure I was suited to the career I had—nothing in my background had really prepared me for how to handle it. I'm so grateful that most of the time I was able to keep it at arm's length. "Take your work seriously," I used to tell my students at IU, "but don't take *yourself* seriously"—that's a road that's going to run out on you, sooner or later. I never really listened to my records much. Now I listen to them once in awhile, and you know what? I wasn't bad! Who knew? If I'd known I was that good, I would have had Bob Reagan ask for more money.

Much as I loved singing, the best part about it was coming

home. All that work wouldn't have meant a thing to me if I hadn't had Bob, Robbie, and Kathleen there for all those years, waiting for me to walk through the door. Those absences were tough on all of us—it killed me to be away when Kathleen had her first communion, or when she had her tonsils removed. If I had it to do all over again, I probably wouldn't have been away from home as much as I was. Thank God we had all those wonderful uninterrupted summers in Maine together.

One night not too long ago, I was lying in bed listening to the radio. An old Bart Howard song came on—"It Was Worth It." Mabel Mercer used to sing it at Tony's, and as I lay there listening, I could still hear the way she got across those wonderful words:

> All in all, it was worth it—
> Oh, that's what I'll say
> To the ladies the very first day
> They discover my first bit of gray.
> All in all, it was worth it . . .

Well—yes. It sure as hell was.

Selected Discography

Opera and Concert Music

Bach: Arias
The Bach Aria Group
From Cantata no. 205, "Der zufriedengesellte Aeolus"; from Cantata
no. 115, "Mache dich, meine Geist, bereit"
Decca DL 9408, Stereo DL 79408

Bach: Cantatas
The Bach Aria Group
No. 68, "Mein glaubiges Herze"; no. 63, "Gott, du hast es wohl
gefüget"; no. 187, "Gott versoget alles Leben"
Decca DL 9405, Stereo DL 79405

Bach: Vocal Selections
The Bach Aria Group
Cantata no. 58, "Ach Gott, wie manches Herzeleid"; Aria from Can-
tata no. 202, "Weichet nur, betrübte Schatten"
Decca DL 9411, Stereo DL 79411

Beethoven: *Missa Solemnis*
New York Philharmonic, Leonard Bernstein, conductor
Carol Smith, contralto; Richard Lewis, tenor; Kim Borg, bass
Westminster Chorus
(also includes Beethoven's *Fantasy for Piano, Chorus, and Orchestra*, op.

80, Rudolf Serkin, piano; Haydn, *Theresia Mass,* Hob. XXII:12,
London Symphony Chorus and Orchestra)
Columbia SM2K 47522

Beethoven: Symphony no. 9 (Choral)
NBC Symphony Orchestra, Arturo Toscanini, conductor
RCA Victor LM 6009 (reissued on SYMP 1230)

Berg: *Wozzeck* (Complete)
New York Philharmonic, Dimitri Mitropoulos, conductor
Columbia SL 118 (reissued on Sony MH2K 62759)

Cherubini: *Medea* (Excerpts)
Columbia Symphony Orchestra, Arnold Gamson, conductor
Columbia ML 5325, Stereo MS 6032
(Slated for CD reissue 1999)

Donizetti: *Maria Stuarda*
Alldis Choir; London Philharmonic, Aldo Ceccato, conductor
Beverly Sills, soprano; Stuart Burrows, tenor; Louis Quilico, baritone
ABC Records ABC ATS-20010

Grieg: *Peer Gynt*—**Incidental Music**
Boston Pops Orchestra, Arthur Fiedler, conductor
RCA Victor LM 2125, Stereo LSC 2125

Handel: *Messiah* (Complete)
Philadelphia Orchestra, Eugene Ormandy, conductor
Martha Lipton, mezzo-soprano; William Warfield, bass-baritone
Columbia M2L 263, Stereo M2S 607

Herbert: *The Red Mill*
Orchestra and chorus directed by Jay Blackton
Wilbur Evans, Felix Knight

Selections from *Babes in Toyland*
Decca DL 8458

Puccini Arias

Columbia Symphony, Max Rudolf, conductor
O mio babbino caro (*Gianni Schicchi*); Musetta's Waltz (*La Bohème*);
Mi chiamano Mimì (*La Bohème*); Donde lieta usci (*La Bohème*); Non
la sospiri (*Tosca*); Vissi d'arte (*Tosca*); Spira sul mare (*Madama Butterfly*);
Un bel dì (*Madama Butterfly*); In quelle trine morbide (*Manon Lescaut*);
Tu che di gel sei cinta (*Turandot*); In questa reggia (*Turandot*)
Columbia ML 5483, Stereo MS 6150

Romberg: *Up in Central Park*

Orchestra conducted by Max Meth
Celeste Holm, Wilbur Evans
Decca 23406 (7276A1)

Vaughan Williams: *Serenade to Music*

New York Philharmonic, Leonard Bernstein, conductor
(also includes Vaughan Williams's Symphony no. 4, *Fantasia on a
Theme by Thomas Tallis, Fantasia on "Greensleeves"*)
Columbia SMK 47638

Verdi Arias

Columbia Symphony, Max Rudolf, conductor
Ritorna vincitor! (*Aida*); Ma dall'arido stelo divulsa (*Un ballo in
maschera*); Salce, salce (*Otello*); Ave Maria (*Otello*); Come in quest'ora
bruna (*Simon Boccanegra*); Tacea la notte placida (*Il trovatore*); D'amor
sull'ali rosee (*Il trovatore*); Pace, pace, mio Dio! (*La forza del destino*)
Columbia ML 5654, Stereo MS 6524
(Selections from this LP reissued on CD as *Eileen Farrell Sings Verdi,*
Sony Classical MHK 62358)

Great Duets from Verdi Operas with Eileen Farrell and Richard Tucker

Columbia Symphony, Fausto Cleva, conductor

Richard Tucker, tenor

Io vengo a domandar (*Don Carlo*); Pur ti riveggo (*Aida*); Vieni a mirar (*Simon Boccanegra*); Teco io sto (*Un ballo in maschera*); Già nella notte densa (*Otello*)

Columbia ML 5606, Stereo MS 6296

(Selections from this LP reissued on CD as *Eileen Farrell Sings Verdi*, Sony Classical MHK 62358)

Wagner: Prelude and Liebestod (*Tristan und Isolde*), *Wesendonck* Songs, Immolation Scene (*Götterdämmerung*)

New York Philharmonic, Leonard Bernstein, conductor (also includes Wagner's Overture to *Tannhäuser*)

Columbia SMK 47644

Wagner: Prelude and Liebestod (*Tristan und Isolde*), Immolation Scene (*Götterdämmerung*)

Boston Symphony Orchestra, Charles Munch, conductor

RCA Victor LM 2255, Stereo LSC 2255

Wagner: *Siegfried* Excerpts

Rochester Philharmonic Orchestra, Erich Leinsdorf, conductor

RCA Victor LM 1066

(This recording and the one following were originally released as separate 78 rpm albums; they were later combined on one RCA Victor LP.)

Wagner: *Wesendonck* Lieder

Leopold Stokowski and His Symphony Orchestra

RCA Victor LM 1066

Arias in the Great Tradition

Columbia Symphony, Max Rudolf, conductor

Beethoven, Ah, Perfido! and Abscheulicher, wo eilst du hin? (*Fidelio*);

Cherubini, Solo un pianto (*Medea*); Gluck, Grands dieux! (*Alceste*);
Weber, Leise, leise and Cavatina (*Der Freischütz*)
Columbia ML 5408, Stereo MS 6086

Eileen Farrell in Grand Opera

Philharmonia Orchestra, Thomas Schippers, conductor
Gluck, Divinités du Styx (*Alceste*); Weber, Ocean, du Ungeheuer!
(*Oberon*); Verdi, Ernani involami! (*Ernani*); Ponchielli, Suicidio! (*La
gioconda*); Massenet, Il est doux, il est bon (*Hérodiade*); Tchaikovsky,
Adieu, forêts (*Jeanne d'Arc*); Debussy, Air de Lia (*L'enfant prodigue*);
Menotti, To This We've Come (*The Consul*)
Angel 35589
(Reissued on CD, with selections from *Eileen Farrell in Songs and Ballads*, as *Eileen Farrell Sings Opera Arias & Songs*, Testament SBT-1073)

Farrell and Tucker: Puccini and Verdi Favorites

Un bel dì (*Madama Butterfly*); Che gelida manina; Mi chiamano Mimì
(*La Bohème*); Nessun dorma; In questa reggia (*Turandot*); E lucevan le
stelle; Vissi d'arte (*Tosca*); La donna e mobile (*Rigoletto*); Ritorna
vincitor; Pur ti riveggo (*Aida*)
Columbia ML 6004; Stereo MS 6604

Song Recital

George Trovillo, piano
Schubert, An die Leier; Die Fischerweise; An die Laute; Du Liebst
mich nicht; Dem Unendlichen; Schumann, Volksliedchen; An den
Mond; Mein schöner Stern; Die Soldatenbraut; Debussy, Beau soir;
C'est l'extase; Fleur des blés; Noël des enfants qui n'ont plus de
maisons; L'ombre des arbres; Poulenc, L'hôtel; Voyage à Paris; C;
Reines des mouettes; Fleurs
Columbia ML 5485, Stereo MS 6151

The Voice of Eileen Farrell

Excerpts from the sound track of the M-G-M film *Interrupted Melody*
M-G-M Records E-3984

Popular Music

Eileen Farrell: Here

Here; How Beautiful Is Night; In the Wee Small Hours of the Morning; Nightfall; Quiet Nights of Quiet Stars; Like Someone in Love; On a Cold Winter Night; The Lamp Is Low; Wasn't It a Lovely Evening?; How High the Moon; A Nightingale Sang in Berkeley Square; Nightmood

Elba 5008-2

Eileen Farrell: It's Over

Arranged and conducted by Robert Farnon

I Get the Blues When It Rains; How About Me?; I'm Through with Love; I'll Remember April; Easy to Remember; Whenever a Soft Rain Falls; Where Do You Start?; Gone with the Wind; The Shining Sea; I'm So Lost; Lush Life; By Myself

Reference RR-46CD

Eileen Farrell: Love Is Letting Go

Arranged and conducted by Robert Farnon

Just in Time; Why Did I Choose You?; Love Is Letting Go; I've Never Been in Love Before; Country Boy; Where Were You This Afternoon?; Every Day; I Dream of You; A Quiet Thing; Time after Time; My Love Turned Me Down Today; Then I'll Be Tired of You; For Eileen

DRG 91436

Eileen Farrell: This Time It's Love

Arranged and conducted by Robert Farnon

Easy to Love; The More I See You; My Foolish Heart; What Is There to Say?; The Nearness of You; More Than You Know; Put Your Dreams Away; Alone Together; My Romance; A Game for Two; Love Dance; The Music That Makes Me Dance; Everything I Love

Reference RR-42CD

Eileen Farrell—with Much Love
With the Loonis McGlohon Quartet
While We're Young; Since I Fell for You; Songbird; On Second
Thought; So Many Stars; Some Other Time; Spring; Here's That
Rainy Day/Bachianas Brasileiras, No. 5; Love; A Child Is Born; Soon
It's Gonna Rain/Come In from the Rain; Indian Summer; Come to
Me; When the World Was Young/Once Upon a Summertime
Audiophile ACD-237

Eileen Farrell Sings Alec Wilder
It's a Fine Day for Walkin' Country Style; It's So Peaceful in the
Country; Moon and Sand; Blackberry Winter; If Someday Comes
Ever Again; Be a Child; Where Do You Go?; Lovers and Losers; The
Lady Sings the Blues; The Worm Has Turned; Where's That
Heartache?; Gonna Be a Cold, Cold Day; Who Can I Turn To?;
I'll Be Around
Reference RR-36CD

Eileen Farrell Sings Harold Arlen
Let's Fall in Love; Out of This World; I Wonder What Became of
Me; I've Got the World on a String; Like a Straw in the Wind; Down
with Love; Happiness Is a Thing Called Joe; A Woman's Prerogative;
Come Rain or Come Shine; Little Drops of Rain/Over the Rain-
bow; When the Sun Comes Out; As Long as I Live; My Shining
Hour; Last Night When We Were Young
Reference RR-30CD

Eileen Farrell Sings Johnny Mercer
Too Marvelous for Words; Skylark; I'm Shadowing You; Moon
River; I Remember You; Laura; You Grow Sweeter as the Years Go
By; I'm Old-Fashioned; I Thought about You; Weekend of a Private
Secretary; Day In, Day Out; Early Autumn; Autumn Leaves
Reference RR-44CD

Eileen Farrell Sings Rodgers & Hart

I Could Write a Book; I Wish I Were in Love Again; Wait Till You See Him; I Didn't Know What Time It Was; Love Me Tonight; Nobody's Heart; It Never Entered My Mind; Mountain Greenery; Sing For Your Supper; Can't You Do a Friend a Favor; Lover; My Heart Stood Still; Little Girl Blue; You're Nearer
Reference RR-32CD

Eileen Farrell Sings Torch Songs

Stormy Weather; When Your Lover Has Gone; 'Round Midnight; The End of a Love Affair; Guess I'll Hang My Tears Out to Dry; Something Cool; I Get Along without You Very Well; Spring Can Really Hang You Up the Most; Black Coffee; Don't Explain; Get Out of Town; This Time the Dream's on Me
Reference RR-34CD

Frank Sinatra Trilogy: Past, Present & Future

Eileen Farrell sings "For the Good Times" with Sinatra
Reprise 2300-2

Here I Go Again

Orchestra conducted by Luther Henderson
Funny Valentine; In Other Words; I Got It Bad and That Ain't Good; Somebody Loves Me; Dreamy; Wrap Your Troubles in Dreams; The Man I Love; Solitaire; To Be in Love; A Foggy Day; The Second Time Around; Taking a Chance on Love
Columbia CL 1653, Stereo CS 8256
(Selections from this LP reissued on CD as *I Gotta Right to Sing the Blues,* Sony Masterworks MDK 47255)

I've Got a Right to Sing the Blues

Orchestra conducted by Luther Henderson
Blues in the Night; I'm Old Fashioned, Supper Time; Looking for a Boy; Glad to Be Unhappy; On the Sunny Side of the Street; Old

Devil Moon; He Was Too Good to Me; Ten Cents a Dance; Ev'ry
Time; September Song; I Gotta Right to Sing the Blues
Columbia CL 1465, Stereo CS 8256
(Selections from this LP reissued on CD as *I Gotta Right to Sing the
Blues,* Sony Masterworks MDK 47255)

The Magnificent Voice of Eileen Farrell: Songs America Loves
London Festival Orchestra and Chorus, Robert Sharples, conductor
You'll Never Walk Alone; Bless This House; Nobody Knows de
Trouble I've Seen; I Got Dat Feeling; Climb Every Mountain; If I
Could Tell You; If I Loved You; Trees; We Shall Overcome; The
Lord's Prayer; Deep River; Peace of Mind
London 5920 mono

Rodgers: *The Sound of Music*
Cincinnati Pops Orchestra, Erich Kunzel, conductor
Frederica von Stade, Håkan Hagegård, Barbara Daniels
Telarc Digital CD 80162

This Fling Called Love
Percy Faith and His Orchestra
Hello, Young Lovers; My Romance; In the Still of the Night; Stormy
Weather; Out of This World; I Never Has Seen Snow; I've Got You
under My Skin; Where or When; The April Age; The Party's Over;
The Faraway Part of Town; Can't Help Lovin' Dat Man
Columbia CL 1739 mono

Together with Love
André Previn, piano, and the André Previn Orchestra
But Not for Me; Spring Is Here; Everywhere I Look; A Sleepin' Bee; I
Wonder What Became of Me; By Myself; Cabin in the Sky; Just for Now;
Where I Wonder; The Morning After; Be My All; Love Is Here to Stay
Columbia CL 1920

Traditional Music

Eileen Farrell in Songs and Ballads
George Trovillo, piano
There Should Be More Joy (Nordoff); To the Children (Rachmaninoff); The Pasture (Naginski); Hickory Hill (Sargent); Sing to Me, Sing (Homer); Through the Years (Youmans); Let My Song Fill Your Heart (Charles); When I Have Sung My Songs (Charles); Summertime (Gershwin); Danny Boy; Down in the Salley Gardens; The Leprechaun (Irish airs)
Angel 35608
(Selections from this LP reissued on CD, along with arias from *Eileen Farrell in Grand Opera*, on *Eileen Farrell Sings Opera Arias & Songs*, Testament SBT-1073)

Carols for Christmas
Orchestra conducted by Luther Henderson
O Come, All Ye Faithful; Away in a Manger; Coventry Carol; Deck the Halls with Boughs of Holly; Sleep, Holy Babe; Snow in the Street; Silent Night; What Child Is This?; O Little Town of Bethlehem; Hark! The Herald Angels Sing; Lullay My Liking; It Came upon a Midnight Clear; The First Noel; God Rest Ye Merry, Gentlemen; Joy to the World; Song of the Crib
Columbia ML 5565, Stereo MS 6165
(Reissued on CD, Sony SFK 60802)

Irish Songs
Columbia Concert Orchestra, Charles Lichter, conductor
Believe Me If All Those Endearing Young Charms; The Minstrel Boy; The Last Rose of Summer; The Kerry Dance; Come Back to Erin; Killarney; Danny Boy; The Rose of Tralee
Columbia M-662 (4-record set, 10-inch 78 rpms)